ADVANCE PRAISE FOR *THE UNLIKELY THRU-HIKER*

"Even for a skilled hiker, a 2,192-mile thru-hike is challenging—so for Derick, much can and will go wrong on the Appalachian Trail. Yet his story takes us into a world where his lack of AT knowledge, his unique perspective, his appearance, and his sense of humor open the minds and hearts of those he encounters along the way.

"Change has come, and the AT will never be the same again. Neither will this unlikely thru-hiker."

–Jennifer Pharr Davis
author, speaker, and hiker who, in 2011, claimed the
fastest known time for finishing the Appalachian Trail,
making her the first woman to earn the record

"Forget what you know or think you know about hiking the Appalachian Trail and experience it through the fresh perspective of novice Derick 'Mr. Fabulous' Lugo, who provides a candid and clear-eyed account of a contemporary thru-hike with engaging humility. His respect for the trail and interactions with other hikers are exemplary."

–David Miller,
author of *AWOL on the Appalachian Trail*
and *The A.T. Guide*

THE UNLIKELY THRU-HIKER

An Appalachian Trail Journey

DERICK LUGO

Appalachian Mountain Club Books
Boston, Massachusetts

AMC is a nonprofit organization, and sales of AMC Books fund our mission of protecting the Northeast outdoors. If you appreciate our efforts and would like to become a member or make a donation to AMC, visit outdoors.org, call 800-372-1758, or contact us at Appalachian Mountain Club, 10 City Square, Boston, MA 02129.

outdoors.org/books-maps

Cover design by Jon Lavalley
Interior design by Eric Edstam

Library of Congress Cataloging-in-Publication Data

Names: Lugo, Derick, author.
Title: The unlikely thru-hiker : an Appalachian Trail journey / Derick Lugo.
Description: Boston, Massachusetts : Appalachian Mountain Club Books, [2019]
Identifiers: LCCN 2019022639 (print) | LCCN 2019022640 (ebook) | ISBN
   9781628421200 (mobi) | ISBN 9781628421194 (epub) | ISBN 9781628421187
   (paperback)
Subjects: LCSH: Lugo, Derick. | Hikers--Appalachian Trail—Biography. |
   Hiking—Appalachian Trail—Anecdotes. | Appalachian Trail—Description and
   travel.
Classification: LCC GV199.92.L84 (ebook) | LCC GV199.92.L84 A3 2019 (print) |
   DDC 796.510974--dc23
LC record available at https://lccn.loc.gov/2019022639

The paper used in this publication meets the minimum requirements of the American National Standard for Information Sciences-Permanence of Paper for Printed Library Materials, ANSI Z39.48-1984. ∞

Outdoor recreation activities by their very nature are potentially hazardous. This book is not a substitute for good personal judgment and training in outdoor skills. Due to changes in conditions, use of the information in this book is at the sole risk of the user. The author and the Appalachian Mountain Club assume no liability for accidents happening to, or injuries sustained by, readers who engage in the activities described in this book.

Interior pages and cover are printed on responsibly harvested paper stock certified by The Forest Stewardship Council®, an independent auditor of responsible forestry practices. Printed in the United States of America, using vegetable-based inks.

10 9 8 7 6 5 4 3   22 23 24 25 26

Dedicated to all the Unlikelies everywhere

CONTENTS

Part 3: Mr. Fabulous

Part 4: New Summits

PROLOGUE

As dusk settles in and steals what little light is left, I feel an uneasiness creep in. I'm futilely attempting to suppress my insecurity about being alone in a forest gone pitch black, but I'm convinced the trees conceal besieging predators.

Was that a big-headed alien behind that pine? What's that noise? Come out. I know you're there.

I hate being out here alone this late in the evening, but after spending the day avoiding a broken ankle in the rocky state of Pennsylvania—Rocksylvania, to those who hike it—I am reaching a much-needed water source hours later than anticipated. I now find myself smack-dab in the middle of the opening scene from *The Evil Dead*, and I'm less than thrilled about being the first character killed off.

As I climb the steep hill to the stream, the rock scree below my feet sends me sliding to the left and then the right, as if it's trying to will me in a different direction. With flip-flops on, it's nearly impossible to avoid looking like I'm just learning how to walk, or slide—or slide-walk.

Below me on the trail I spot a large, dark object that stops me dead in my tracks. I hold my breath and tell myself not to make a sound, but I know, somehow, that it senses my presence. I squint, hoping what I'm seeing is a fallen tree or some crazy figment of my imagination. But it's still there, large and boulder-shaped. In this light, or lack of it, it looks brown. I have not moved or blinked in over a minute, and my ears are as sharp as a bat's, but neither of us makes a sound. All of a sudden, the boulder-shaped object raises its arms, lifts up its slumped head, and turns to reveal a bear's snout.

Damn it, my entire being cries.

I'm about half a dozen yards away, and the steep hill has placed me almost on top of the mammal. I hear a scream—and yes, it's mine. The scream morphs into a squeal, one that I will never admit having made to anyone. It's also possible that I soil my shorts, but that is something I'll have to confirm later. For now, there's a huge bear less than 20 feet away, so I turn, only to slip on the rock scree, causing my right flip-flop to slide from under my toes and up along my ankle, like an anklet. I scramble hand and foot up the hill, sliding farther backward the more I exert my energies forward, like someone running on a gravel treadmill or in a nightmare, trying to claw my way from an unforeseen threat.

Don't run, fool, says the inner voice I never listen to in situations like this. *Stand your ground. Make your presence dominant. It will certainly flee*, the voice commands.

But I know better. I know what's in store for me. The bear is not going anywhere, and I'm not going to scare it away.

In fact, I may have just lured him into our camp.

I look up in the direction that leads to my unsuspecting trail family, and then I start to run with all my might.

A few seconds later, I enter the camp, yelling breathlessly, "We've got company! We've got company!"

Part 1

WHY THE AT?

CHAPTER 1

AT, Short for the Appalachian Trail

I'm in New York City, staying with Nina and her husband, Gene, in their Central Park West apartment for a few weeks. I've known this couple for several years, long enough for us to share many memories.

Our friendship started when Nina and I worked together in the city at a comedy club. Back then we feigned our dislike for rookie comedians and their gleeful exuberance in trying their luck on the stage. We made fun of their bombed efforts then turned around and encouraged them to continue trying.

"I'm doing the AT!" I say excitedly as I emerge from their guest bedroom. Nina is sitting on the living room sofa with a cup of coffee, watching a recorded episode of *Saturday Night Live*.

"Great! What's an AT?" Nina replies as she leans over to the remote and pauses the program.

"The AT. It's short for the Appalachian Trail," I say, hoping this might ring a bell for her.

"Oh. What's an Appa-la-sia Trail?" she says absentmindedly, staring at the frozen picture on the TV screen.

Did she deliberately mispronounce it?

It's not her lack of familiarity with the Appalachian Trail that annoys me. What bothers me is the way she says it, with a distinct lack of interest.

Doesn't she see how stoked I am?

Normally I get a kick out of her snappy remarks, but now my enthusiasm for the AT has been deflated by her indifference. She is either totally clueless or is just disregarding the whole idea. Sometimes with Nina, it's hard to tell the two apart. Her hard New York exterior can be a bit much.

"Really? It's a long-distance hike from Georgia to Maine, through the Appalachian Mountains."

I wait for a response as she scrunches her face, trying to make sense of what I just told her.

"OK . . . why would you want to do that?" she says, frowning.

"What? Because I can, because I've never done anything like this before," I say.

Is she messing with me?

The similarity in our humor is the glue that bonds our friendship, but now . . . I don't get it. Or maybe I don't want to. At this moment, all I want is some validation or encouragement from my friend.

"It's an adventure, something I've wanted to do for a while."

"You've never mentioned it before," she shoots back, as if catching me in a lie.

"I'm sure I did. Look, that's not the point. I'm hik—"

"What are you going to eat? Will you have cell service, so you can order food? Do they deliver out there?" She barrages me with questions, ignoring my efforts to explain.

"I will bring a cell for when I'm in town resupplying and if there's an emergency. I'll be on top of mountains, which I think will be outside of delivery and maybe cell service," I say, not truthfully knowing the answer.

"Hmm, I don't know about this. How long will it take you?" she asks, unable to grasp the thought of me doing something so out of character.

"I'm going to try to do it in five months," I say proudly.

"You're going to live in the mountains for five months?" she repeats, squinting her eyes at me, as if I were too far away for her to see.

Before I can answer, she continues. "Listen, pretty boy, I know you. You are the most well-groomed, metrosexual black man in New York City. You, in the woods, without your mirror, your beauty products, or your designer clothes? *Please!* How will you shower?"

"Wait, I don't have beauty products. OK. Maybe lotions."

"What about the manicures?"

"Hmph . . . OK, I get manicures once in a while."

"What abou—"

"OK, OK, I get it," I say, wanting to finally get my point across before she convinces me I'm too meticulous about my appearance to live out in the woods.

"Look," I begin to explain again, "I'll shower in towns, about once a week. But, I ca—"

"Once a week?" She cuts me off again. "You're gonna be dirty for a whole week? I don't believe it!"

What she doesn't understand is that although some thru-hikers, as end-to-end trail hikers are called, are known for their overgrown beards and their natural, earthy smells, that's a matter of individual choice. To some, it's a chance to let go, to shed their everyday routines alongside societal notions about acceptable appearances and smells. For some hikers, that's part of the backpacking experience, especially on a long-distance journey. But it's not for me.

"No, I'm not going to be dirty for a whole week. What I was about to say is that I can wash up every day at a stream, a brook, or whatever water source I can find. Shoot, I can give myself a birdbath in a puddle if I have to. Trust me when I tell you that I'm going to be the cleanest, prettiest hiker on the trail."

"Ha! Pretty? For who? Aren't you going to be in the rural South?" she says with a smirk.

"Yeah, and?" I respond.

Where's she going with this?

"What, you tryin' to mate with a bear?"

"Well, perhaps proper grooming isn't strictly necessary on the trail," I say, finally stumped by her remarks.

"Dude, you know what?" Nina asks, standing up, with her right index finger pointing up, her eyes wide and eager. She's got that look I know so well. A thought has crossed her mind that she is dying to share.

"What's that?" I say, apprehensive of what may come next.

"Slick your dreads with honey. That will attract them to ya," she says with a dopey grin.

I'm not impressed.

She jerks her head like a wild animal at Gene as he passes by the living room on his way to the kitchen for his morning cup of coffee. "Hey, Gene, pretty boy here has gone wild."

"What?" Gene says with indifference.

"Derick is doing an AT!" she shouts to her husband.

"Derick is joining an A-Team?" he shouts back from the kitchen.

"No, I'm hiking the AT! What's an A-Team?" I shout, needlessly, because everyone else is.

What's going on here?

The three of us seem to be having different conversations.

"I don't know. I was going to ask you the same thing," Gene says as he returns from the kitchen with his coffee.

I stare at him for a moment, feeling my left eyebrow rise. Lack of sleep and this merry-go-round conversation with Nina and Gene has left me exhausted. Caffeine in my system will make it all better.

"Remember that show *The A-Team*?" Gene asks Nina as I pour a cup of joe.

I close my eyes, slowly shake my head, and let out a long sigh.

Actually hiking the AT has got to be easier than explaining it to these two.

CHAPTER 2

Difficulty . . . Strenuous

It's March 19, 2012, 7:40 a.m., and I'm the first to arrive at the Amicalola Falls State Park visitor center. The center doesn't open for another twenty minutes, but I'm eager to see the stone arch, our gateway to the approach trail, which in turn will lead me to the start of the Appalachian Trail. I make my way around to the back of the center.

. . . and there it is.

I place my backpack down on one of the six long benches. It's strange to finally be here. An overwhelming sense of apprehension threatens to overtake me. I'm suddenly, intensely aware of my Appalachian Trail ignorance and how little I know about surviving in the wilderness.

Does my inexperience shine on my forehead like a giant Times Square billboard? Will it be obvious I have no idea what I'm doing? What did I get myself into?

I push my doubts aside and try to replace them with thoughts of what I *do* know: that I'm in awe of finally being here. The stone path leading through the popular archway smacks me with a dose of reality. This is no pipe dream. I'm actually embarking on a long-distance hike.

It's real. I'm finally here. And I'm scared.

"Hey," I hear someone say behind me, snapping me out of my moment.

I turn around to see a white-haired yet lean and youthful man. He was on the same Amtrak train I arrived on this morning. Close behind him are two other guys, seemingly ready to start their thru-hikes as well.

I return the first man's greeting. He introduces himself as L-Dog, short for Laughing Dog. A cool trail name, but to me, he looks more like a college professor and not the rapper his trail name implies. From what I've seen online, trail names are usually given to thru-hikers by other thru-hikers, as a way of identifying each other. We leave our old life behind for a new life on the trail, sort of a rebirth—thus, the need for a new name. Trail names also seem to be easier to recall than a person's name. I could easily remember a name like L-Dog instead of Lenny or Lawrence. But whoever dubbed this tenured faculty member L-Dog must be really bad at giving out names.

The two other guys with him introduce themselves. I shake hands with Mike, who has an easygoing aura about him, as if this is going to be a walk in the park for him. The other fella, Stephane, is from Switzerland. He's quiet— maybe shy or perhaps measuring his words. This place is foreign to me and I'm from this country, so I can't imagine how it all feels for him.

The visitor center doors unlock and we enter, look around, and sign a register for thru-hikers beginning at this point of the trail. I'm the 438th hiker to start this season.

It's as good a number as any.

I must remember to call my mother and give her this number. She believes any three-digit number that appears during your day is a lucky one. She'll want to play 438 in a lottery or something.

It occurs to me the lady behind the counter may be able to answer some of my novice questions, so I go ahead and bombard her. She responds graciously. She also confirms that the thru-hike completion rate is about 25 percent, reinforcing my determination to beat the odds. I wonder how many of the 75 percent who didn't make it felt as optimistic as I do now.

"I just weighed my pack," I hear someone say.

"Where?" I quickly ask, remembering I want to check the weight of my backpack.

"There's a hanging scale with a hook up front," L-Dog says.

L-Dog. I'm having trouble picturing him as L-Dog. I want to change his trail name to *Professor Digory Kirke*.

I grab my backpack and head for the scale. I've read that a comfortable and safe weight for a backpack is about 25 percent of an individual's weight. I'm hoping to go somewhat light, around 30 pounds.

My pack weighs 42 pounds.

What the fu—rther!

Josh, another hiker who just arrived with his parents, helps me lift my pack off the scale. I've been revealed as one of those who overpacks. From what I've heard, this is not unusual.

"That's about the same as mine," Josh says.

"Really? I was hoping it would be way lighter. It feels like I'm carrying a load of cinder blocks," I say, bewildered.

Knowing my pack's actual weight has triggered something in my brain that, I fear, will make the load feel even heavier. Josh finds my shock funny. He laughs before sharing some words of encouragement: "It'll get lighter as you figure out what you need. At Neels Gap you can get some help deciding what you can do without."

He explains that an outfitter, Mountain Crossing at Neels Gap, here in Georgia, employs experienced and knowledgeable staff members who can go through my heavy pack and tell me why carrying four hardcover books, two weeks of food, and a large NYPD flashlight/bludgeon that takes four D batteries is a bad idea. Of course, I didn't bring any of those items. Well, I may have overdone it with the ready-to-eat Indian meals. The water in those packets is making them quite heavy.

I must remember to eat them first.

Oh, and the 24 pouches of tuna and salmon, twenty of which I'm beginning to think are completely unnecessary.

"Yeah, you're right," I say, aiming for positivity. With a grunt, I lift my sack of cannonballs and head back to the benches behind the visitor center.

"Take the left trail up the steps. It's far easier," someone says.

I've heard the demanding approach trail causes many thru-hikers to quit before they even get started. It's like an immediate weeding-out: If the approach trail is too much to handle, don't bother continuing on.

Sounds like a challenge. I like those.

Besides, I made no alternate plan for the next five to six months. I don't really have any choice but to complete this hike from Georgia to Maine, so a few steps are not going to change that.

"Damn, these steps are murder," I hear myself say to no one in particular, twenty excruciating minutes later.

What did I expect after seeing a warning sign that read:

DIFFICULTY . . . STRENUOUS 175 STEPS

... then another one that read:

DIFFICULTY . . . STRENUOUS 425 STEPS

Have I ever climbed 600 steps before with a 42-pound pack strapped to my back? *Hell to the NO!*

Neither Swiss (which is what I decide to call my new hiking friend, being that he's from Switzerland, but mostly because I can't remember his real name) nor I knew what to expect when together we passed through the stone archway at the head of the approach trail.

I'm uncertain how to use my trekking poles. There seemed to be no reason to use them on the paved portion of the trail we were walking on earlier, but I want to figure out how they work before I really need them. Does the left pole go forward as my right foot goes forward or vice versa?

Am I overthinking this?

Swiss takes the lead up the first set of steps. Only a few steps in, I know I'm in trouble, but Swiss looks as if he's riding an escalator. Trying not to show my immediate fatigue, I push on.

I shouldn't be this out of shape, I think.

I run 10 miles a day in Central Park, in 90-degree weather, and I look good doing it.

What forces are at work here? OK, I have to stop soon. Oh, a waterfall.

A good excuse to pause. I pull out my camera and take a couple of shots, admiring the falling water—or so it seems. In reality, I'm trying to suck in as much air as I possibly can without giving away that I'm about to pass out into the waterfall and be done with this journey.

Hell, it technically hasn't even started.

The approach trail is not even part of the AT. Still, I don't care what others say: My body disagrees. I look down at the sinister, air-stealing steps I've already traveled and then up at the many more to come. I drop my head and push on.

To make matters worse, Swiss still looks as if he's enjoying a stroll through an art gallery or browsing a department store.

What the heck?!

After several quick breaks, we finally make it up to the last step. "Why did you make me do this?" I ask Swiss breathlessly.

"I just met you. I made you do nothing," he responds.

"Well, you should have known better. Hey, let's not do that again, OK? Is that Mike?" I ask, as we enter the parking lot at the top of the falls.

We see Mike sitting on a low stone wall next to a public restroom. He left about ten minutes before Swiss and I, the first of our new friends to pass through the stone arch and start up those evil steps. Now he's relaxing, as if he's done for the day.

"Hey, Mike, looks like a good spot for a break," I say, glad to be able to take my pack off.

Swiss does the same.

"Yeah, my cell battery is low, so I'm charging it in the restroom," Mike says while snacking on an energy bar.

I dig his laid-back attitude.

Just then a car pulls into the parking lot and out jumps Josh. He grabs his bag from the back of his parents' SUV, shares a long goodbye with them, and starts walking toward us.

"What the—did you skip the 600 STRENUOUS steps?" I ask with amazement.

Josh smiles. "Yeah, I was going to have my parents drive up with my pack while I hiked up the steps, but I didn't want them to have to wait for me, so I rode up with them."

"Yo, those steps were a breeze. You should have taken them," I say, shooting a glare at the wicked steps below us.

"Oh really?" Swiss responds, rolling his eyes.

"No, it was far from easy. You're lucky you got the ride up," I say to Josh.

"The AT doesn't start until we reach Springer Mountain anyway," Josh says.

"Nonetheless, my lazy friend, I'm counting it," I say with a wide-eyed smile.

"Ha. Are you guys camping at Springer Mountain Shelter?" Josh asks the three of us.

"I am," I say.

"Yeah, me too," says Swiss.

"I'll be up there," says Cool-Hand-Mike.

"Great. Then I'll see you guys there," Josh says, turning toward the trees, which are marked with blue paint every 100 feet or so.

"I'll see you guys at the shelter," Mike says. "I'm going to wait until my cell is charged."

"Coolio. See ya there." I make a short, guttural sound as I lift my pack.

This has to get easier.

Swiss notices my struggle and comes over to help lift my pack off my shoulder so I can adjust it on my back. He advises that I swing it around in one smooth motion instead of lifting then resetting it.

"That's what . . . I was doing. What . . . you couldn't . . . tell?" I strain to say as I try to lift my pack higher onto my back before locking the chest and waist straps.

The sun is shining through bare tree branches, and although it looks like winter, it feels like a warm spring day.

What!

I jump at the sudden sound of dried leaves crunching under hurried footsteps. I turn to face the sound with alert eyes, and then I see it: a gray, bushy-tailed squirrel running up a tree.

Oh.

That little critter sounded like a stampede of killer wild boars.

I mustn't let my imagination get the best of me out here.

We've been hiking for more than three hours, and I'm still trying to figure out how to swing my poles when we arrive. I see Josh staring at the distant mountains that provide our surroundings' backdrop. He seems to have been here a while.

I scan the area that makes up this mountaintop we're standing on and wonder, *Is this it?* For some reason I thought Springer Mountain would be—I don't know—*bigger.*

This is the actual start of the Appalachian Trail?

I'm not sure what I expected, maybe pyramids or statues of gods or anything but what I'm actually seeing: a large rock with a plaque, another plaque on a rock floor, and a view nearly blocked by branches. That's it.

Hmm.

"OK, forget Katahdin. Springer Mountain is enough. I'm going home," I say, drained and out of breath, as I walk toward the large boulder with a plaque secured to it.

"Don't say that," responds an older woman who's leaning on a nearby tree. She's with a gentleman around her own age, and by his side is another man who appears to be a park ranger.

"I kid. Just a little humor from an exhausted tenderfoot," I say with a tired smile.

"Are you guys starting a thru-hike?" asks the possible park ranger. He's short and skinny, with glasses way too big for his face. Long strands of his hair are combed over to one side, but I can't tell if he's going bald or if he's just sporting a bad hairdo. That aside, he has a friendly face.

"Yeah, we are," I reply.

"At least you're attempting, huh?" asks the woman.

"No, I'm quite sure I'm going all the way," I say politely.

I'm not going to fall into a mindset of *maybe I'll make it*. I already have enough going against me, starting with how clueless I am about the trail. Positive thoughts are my biggest asset out here in the unknown. I could have told her all that, but I'm still collecting as much air as my lungs can muster.

"The goal is Katahdin, nothing less," I add.

"That's the way to think," says her companion.

"So, what I have here are AT matches that I give to all northbound thru-hikers," the maybe-ranger chimes in. "Some keep them as souvenirs, and others take them all the way to Katahdin. For a while, the Appalachian Trail Conservancy gave out gifts to thru-hikers who presented the matches after finishing their hikes. I'm not sure how it works now, but take them with you all the way, and you may be surprised."

"Thanks," I say as he hands me a book of matches. "Are you a park ranger?"

"No, I'm John, the caretaker here at Springer Mountain Shelter," he says.

"You can also grab a small rock from here and take it to Katahdin, as a token of your thru-hike," Josh says, joining us.

"Yeah, but the thing about that is, all the rocks here were brought down from Katahdin by southbound thru-hikers. You'll just be taking them back home," John says with a big grin.

I have a feeling he has told that joke many times before but is just as gleeful to tell it again. I skip the rock tradition, but I keep the matches. You never know. I may need them along the way. While we're chatting, it hits me. I'm here, at the start of the Appalachian Trail. I endured the strenuous steps, and now I'm atop Springer Mountain.

It's all downhill from here, right?

CHAPTER 3

Lessons at Springer Mountain

DAMN IT, WHAT'S WRONG WITH THIS THING?

I have my tent set up under a tree in a grassy area at Springer Mountain Shelter, but I can't seem to get the stakes into the ground. Without them, my tent fly will not stay secure.

Josh must have seen me struggling, because he strolls over with a rock and hammers down all of my stakes with a "that's how you do it" look. I stand there in awe of his genius.

Why didn't I think of that?

"Dude, thanks. That was going to be my next move," I say unconvincingly. "I guess my inexperience is showing, huh?"

"Gotta start somewhere, right?" he says and nonchalantly walks away.

When Josh, Swiss, and I arrived at the shelter around 3 P.M., John, the caretaker, informed us that the camp will be crowded this evening, based on the number of hikers on-trail. We passed a group of high school kids earlier, but as the first to arrive, we have our pick of the tentsites. We find a nice spot 200 yards from the shelter. I put my tent under a tree, near a campfire site that has two long log seats. Swiss is pitching his tent on the other side of the tree, and Josh is on the other side of the campfire. Mike arrives and finds another clearing just outside of our camp circle.

It's not even 4 P.M., and we're all settled in. Josh and Swiss relax against the long logs, talking and going over their Awol guides. There are various types of AT guides, but *The A.T. Guide*—also known as the Awol guide, by David "Awol" Miller—is the one most thru-hikers use. As far as I can tell, it has everything I need to know to hike the AT. It includes mileage and elevation markers; icons to indicate water sources, shelters, and campsites; and maps of towns near the trail where we can resupply, shower, and find cheap hostels for an overnight stay. This guide is one of the most important pieces of gear I carry.

While my companions are planning their hike for tomorrow, I scope out the area. I pass Mike napping on a grassy patch outside his tent.

That dude is so mellow.

I continue toward the caretaker's enormous yellow tent. The cabin-size structure resembles a large inflatable bounce house. A pair of boots and a lawn chair sit outside the entrance. John doesn't seem to lack any luxuries.

Is that a welcome mat? Could there actually be Pottery Barn furniture inside?

I'm tempted to take a peek inside, but I walk over to the shelter instead. Along the way I see steel cables hanging from high up on the trees, like part of a circus trapeze act. These must be the cables campers use to hang food bags, keeping their rations out of a bear's reach.

But how do they work?

I pull on one of the cables, expecting it to reveal its secrets, but nothing happens. I pull another cable. Nothing. I ponder this puzzle as I continue to the shelter.

I chat with a few hikers at the shelter before I head back to camp. On the way, I see a sign for a water source and remind myself I'll have to come back to fill up.

As I approach the campsite, I glance over at the new tent that will be my home for the next five months. I get an achy feeling in my chest, and I feel dizzy with insecurity. I'm already missing New York, and like a frightened child, I want to go home.

Why did I think I could do this?

The question surprises me more than the homesick feeling. I've traveled before, for long periods of time, so why is this any different? Why should I feel so afraid? I look up at the clouds and try to clear my mind.

One way or another, I'm doing this, I muse to myself.

Feeling better, I continue to my tent. I grab my Platypus water bladder, my water pump, and an empty 32-ounce Powerade bottle that I plan to use for a canteen.

I head to the water source, which is a stream with a small pool fed by a white plastic pipe.

As I remove the Katadyn water-filtration pump from its carrying case, it dawns on me that I don't really know how it works. My internet research has given me only the vaguest idea of how to use it.

I *do* know I can use the Katadyn to simultaneously pump and filter water from any stream or brook, rendering the water potable. Water treatment tablets are another option, but they leave an iodine aftertaste. Water treatment drops, such as Aquamira, kill bacteria in water using chlorine dioxide; after half an hour, the water is safe to drink and has no iodine aftertaste.

Another option I looked at is the SteriPen, a purifier that uses ultraviolet light to destroy waterborne microbes. All you have to do is stir the pen in the untreated water, and voilà, the water is drinkable. But like the pills, the pen does not filter debris from the water. Although either would be lighter to carry than the Katadyn pump, the aftertaste, wait time, and debris lost the debate.

Fortunately, the pump is easier to use than I expected. A few pre-pumps to clean out the tubes, and I'm done in no time.

When I return to our campsite, I meet a few new hikers. One of them is a guy with the trail name Dark Age who seems thrilled to finally be on the AT. He's so wildly enthusiastic that I begin to think he's getting paid or being sponsored to hike the trail. This dude is definitely the official spokesman of the Appalachian Trail. If anyone is going to make it all the way to Katahdin, it's this guy.

While listening to the AT enthusiast, I look over at Mike, who is still lying on the grass. His foot is crossed over his knee, and he's looking up at the sky like a man who doesn't have a care in the world. An image of Huckleberry Finn crosses my mind. I follow his gaze. The weather is springlike, and few clouds are in the sky. The sun is shining bright, but it's heading west and will disappear in a few hours. I stroll over to Mellow-Man-Mike.

"Couldn't ask for a better hiking day, huh?" I ask, breaking his reverie.

"Yeah, it's unbelievable. Hope we get the same for the rest of the week," he says as he gazes at the descending sun. "We should get a good view of the sunset today."

Pleased at the thought, I respond, "That'll be a nice end to our day."

Josh joins us and shows me how to gauge when the sun will set.

"Stretch your arm out with your palm facing you and your fingers horizontal. Now, with the top of your hand right under the sun, count how many fingers it takes to get to the horizon. I count six. Each finger represents fifteen minutes, so that's an hour and a half, more or less, when the sun will set."

He smiles at my astonished expression. I must look like someone who has just discovered the secret of eternal life or uncovered a portal to another dimension.

I try it myself, counting my fingers like a child trying to solve a math problem. I shake my head in amazement and thank him for another lesson in outdoor living.

I turn to share this nugget of information with Swiss, but I'm distracted by a group of teenagers who are swarming around us in search of an area to camp. They sound like a gaggle of loud geese.

"That was a tough climb, huh?" I say to one of the kids.

"It was so much fun," she says.

I would have appreciated her enthusiasm if it weren't so dismissive. Plus, it wasn't so much *fun*—it was so much *hard*. Darn whippersnappers.

Maybe it's me. Maybe I'm not hiker-fit yet.

When I wasn't busy gasping for air, I actually enjoyed today's hike. I decide I shouldn't let a dismissive demeanor ruffle my dreadlocks.

With what seems like energy to spare, the pip-squeaks set up camp in an area a few yards from us.

Josh starts a campfire while Mike, Swiss, and I prepare for an early dinner. I'm thrilled to be eating by a fire, like in those old western movies. We're rugged cowboys ready to rustle up some grub, a can of beans or some beef jerky, except there's no can, and I'm a vegetarian. But maybe some tofurkey.

I've been looking forward to this part—not because I'm hungry, but because I'm eager to try out my new mini Trangia stove. Looking to minimize weight, I originally thought I'd skip the stove, but then I considered my coffee addiction. I blame—well, more like thank—my mother for introducing me to *café con leche*, a Latinx drink of strong coffee served with lots of milk. *Mucho* tasty. I'm now accustomed to having coffee to start my day, and a morning without café would be like forgetting to brush my teeth, which I assure you does not happen.

The mini stove I'm using comes with a 0.8-liter aluminum pot, a nonstick pan that also serves as a lid, an alcohol burner, a wind shield, and a pot lifter that looks like large tweezers. The stove is compact; all the parts can be stored in the pot, and the lid snaps shut to secure everything in place.

I lay all of the parts in front of me. I've stored denatured alcohol in a small plastic bottle. I guess at the amount of alcohol I should pour into the burner and hope for the best. With the first strike of my lighter, the flames jump up. I jerk my head back and make a mental note to watch my hands and dreadlocks the next time I attempt to light this ferocious burner. I decide to cook the heaviest meals in my backpack first, so I place a pouch of Indian food in the boiling water.

Meanwhile, Mike spills his dinner. He stares down at the ramen noodles sprawled on the ground, the bowl turned over on top of them. He then looks up at us and nonchalantly scoops the noodles back into the bowl. He begins eating again, as if nothing happened.

Not sure I would have done that. Then again, I may want to think twice before wasting food out here.

"Bravo, Mike," I say. "No shame in eating dirt, bugs, and that slimy thing I see crawling in your bowl. It's not a noodle, buddy."

We all laugh and agree it could have happened to any of us. Still, I'm secretly glad it wasn't me, like the overweight kid who's relieved when the bully picks on the scrawny guy instead.

After dinner, I set out to hang my food bag on the brainteaser bear cables.

"Is it me, or is anyone else having trouble with those mystifying cables?" I ask as I rise to leave.

"Stephane figured it out," Josh says.

"Nah . . . really?"

"I'll show you when I'm finished," Swiss offers.

What?

"Never mind," I say flippantly. "I'll figure it out. But if I'm not back in an hour, send help."

I walk away with an exaggerated swing of my arms to emphasize my confidence.

When I reach the cables, I look up and eyeball the contraption.

What am I missing?

Then I do something I should have done to start with: I reach over to the end of a loop that is latched to a steel eyehook on the tree and release it. When I pull on one side of the loop, the latch rises, and a carabiner lowers. When it reaches me, I hook the carabiner to my food bag. Then I pull on the other side of the loop and watch the bag rise until I'm able to latch the end onto the eyehook on the pole.

There. Bear bag hung.

I congratulate myself and walk back with the proud air of a know-it-all.

"You figured it out?" asks Josh.

"It's what I do. I'm a finder of answers, a solver of mysteries, a decoder, if you will," I say, waving my arms like a model showcasing an item for sale.

Swiss is quick to end my grandstanding. "You just unhooked it from the pole, right?"

"Yeah, I just unhooked it," I say. "It's easy to overthink it, right?"

He doesn't reply.

"Right?" I ask again.

Swiss smirks and shrugs his shoulders.

"Whatever. Let's go see the sunset," I say, noticing the sun sinking toward the horizon.

It's nearly 7 o'clock when we reach the Springer Mountain plaque, where there's a clearing. I bring my headlamp, camera, and a composition book that I'm using as a journal. We sit quietly on the stone top and take in the beauty of the scene. I write a few words in my journal but find it hard to look away from the sky, which is streaked with yellow and orange. When the sun finally disappears over the horizon, the clouds look like a tapestry of fire woven across the sky.

When we return to our campsite, darkness is upon us. We settle by the campfire for our first night on the Appalachian Trail, and my first night ever on a mountain. The moment doesn't last long, though. I quickly begin to get heavy-eyed. It's only 7:30 in the evening, and I'm calling it a night. All that stair climbing has put a beatdown on this night owl.

"Guys, I think I'm done for the day. See ya in the morning," I say as I rise and walk to my tent. "Love you—feel like I've known you my whole life."

As I get myself settled into my tent, I hear, "Eww, this smells awful!" from one of the young hikers camping nearby.

"What does?" someone asks.

"My underwear," she shares shamelessly with us all.

I laugh but then wonder how long will it be before I have the same reaction to my undergarments.

Crawling into my sleeping bag, I pause and look around in my tent at what few possessions I have. It's incredible to think this is all I'll need for the next half-year. I contemplate my first day and feel good about having conquered the unforgiving steps. I think about how comforting it is to have these three guys camping with me and about what I've learned in such a short time. This was a day filled with useful lessons—lessons I hope will help carry me all the way to Katahdin.

CHAPTER 4

Just Follow the Blazes!

DO I HEAR BIRDS?

I gradually wake from a deep sleep.

It's the first day of spring, and I'm being gently awakened by . . . birds. It's a marvelous sound, and I lie still for a moment, taking it in. There's none of the morning city sounds I'm accustomed to: no cars, no construction work outside my window, nothing but the sun brightening the inside of my eyelids—and birds singing somewhere outside of my tent. I slowly open my eyes. The morning sun bathes the inside of my tent in a warm golden glow. I'm amazed that somehow this tent seems more spacious than I recall it being a week ago in my bedroom.

I'm happy, and the birds sing that they are, as well. I have never been awakened by such lovely sounds. To my surprise, I have slept through the night, something I haven't done in a long time. I'm normally up at night, my mind filled with random thoughts. When this happens, I read or write until I'm tired enough to fall back to sleep. I have lived in New York City most of my life and have never slept in a tent. I had no idea what to expect, but I'd predicted I would spend my first night out in the wilderness sleepless and frightened of creepy crawlers and night creatures ready to do me harm. What I expected and what I experienced could not have been more different.

After writing in my journal last night, I wrapped my dreadlocks under my head, which incidentally makes a perfect pillow. Falling asleep out here in the wilderness was easier than I imagined it would be. It's not that I favor the loud sounds and the busyness of the city; it's just that I'm accustomed to those background noises. Yet I closed my weary eyes—and the next thing I know, I'm in a Disney movie, with birds singing all around me. If I step out of this tent, will cartoon birds land on my shoulder and cause me to break out in a Zip-a-Dee-Doo-Dah song, like Uncle Remus in *Song of the South*?

When I do finally step out of my tent, I see that Josh, Swiss, and Mike are already having breakfast. There are no cartoon birds, but the atmosphere is animated. I greet the guys and thank Josh for grabbing my food bag. I sit next to him and begin making my first cup of coffee on the trail. I decided on instant coffee instead of cowboy (which is roasted ground coffee mixed with boiling water), French press, or filtered coffee (which out here means boiling ground coffee then pouring it through a filter). For me, teabag-style instant coffee seems less of a hassle, lighter to carry, and easier to prepare.

"Hey, Derick, we're thinking of going just beyond Hawk Mountain Shelter," Josh says. "That group of teens from last night is hiking to the shelter, and it's going to be packed."

"Oh, OK," I respond.

I had planned to stay at Hawk Mountain Shelter. I knew there would be many thru-hikers and day hikers on the trail at this time of year, but I'm not bothered by the company. In fact, I enjoy meeting new people. But I dig these three and would like to stick with them for a while.

"Well, you guys look like you're ready to get going," I say. "It'll take me a while to figure out how to pack everything into my backpack, so I'll catch up if I can."

"Do you need help?" asks Josh.

This guy rocks. He's always willing to help.

"Nah, I'm fine. Thanks, dude," I say, extending my hand to him and sharing a fist bump.

My three new friends finish their breakfast and begin packing as I prepare to drink my instant coffee.

Eww, it's nasty.

Still, I down it all, grateful to have any type of coffee out here.

When I walk over to my tent, I notice that I accidentally left a bag of trash hanging on a low branch just over my tent. Josh sees me grabbing it.

"Was that left there all night?" he asks.

"Yeah, I forgot about it," I say, a little embarrassed by my blunder.

"You want to put that with your food bag at night," he says.

He's right. By the sound of his tone, I can tell he's concerned that a wild animal could have been attracted by the scent.

"My bad," I say with a half-smile.

He shrugs. "No worries. You'll get it."

I tie up the bag and stuff it into a side pocket of my backpack. Last night I noticed that the guys were sealing their trash in ziplock bags. Another genius move. The plastic shopping bag I'm using has me feeling like a kid sent to school on a rainy day wearing a black trash bag instead of a poncho.

Get hip to it, Derick!

Swiss, Josh, and Mike head out together, but it takes me an extra 45 minutes to break down my tent and neatly get everything into my bag.

"Hey, you're still here?" asks John, the caretaker, as he approaches.

"Yeah, this is all new to me," I say. "I think my pack shrunk overnight, or somehow I have more stuff than I had yesterday. I suspect someone is playing a trick on me," I add as I try to adjust an outside strap on my backpack, the purpose of which I am unsure.

"Need any assistance?" John offers.

"Nah thanks, I think I got it. I'll figure it out eventually," I say.

"You're from New York City, right?" he asks, recalling our conversation yesterday.

"Yeah, I am."

"Man, this must be so different for you!" he exclaims.

"It *is* a different world. It's so unlike anything I've ever done."

I give up on the useless strap, deciding it's probably just for show.

"Sounds like you're stepping out of your comfort zone, huh?"

"Yeah, I guess I am," I say, trying not to sound insecure but suddenly feeling that way.

I look down at all of the gear I'm trying to squeeze into my backpack.

"Well, who knows," I continue. "By putting myself in this situation, I may discover something new about myself."

"I don't doubt you will," he says. "You're in for a great adventure. Good luck, New York."

John extends his hand. I go for it but find it's not a handshake he's after. He reaches down to my backpack and clips the *useless* strap over the top of my bag, securing the top lid. He smiles, but it's not a smug smile. His big glasses and combover do not allow that type of attitude.

Who's useless now? I imagine the strap saying to me with a smirk.

"Thanks, John. You know, you're an OK guy," I say.

"Thanks," he says as he extends his hand again.

I wait a beat for another *Backpack Straps 101* lesson, but this time he actually is offering a handshake. I move my hand a bit too quickly toward his, causing our hands to ram together.

He must think I'm missing a few brain cells.

"Sorry, I thought you were adjusting something else on my bag."

He laughs, and this time he shakes my hand. He then heads to his yellow house-tent. Eventually I get everything into my pack, and an hour after my three hiker friends left camp, I'm finally ready to follow the now-white blazes that will start the first official day of my Appalachian Trail journey. The blazes are long, white, 4-by-6-inch rectangles painted on trees, large rocks, logs, bridges, or any visible object. Their purpose is to guide hikers along the Appalachian Trail.

Leaving the camp area, I make a right onto the AT and follow my first set of white blazes. I place my hand on one as I walk by. Within moments of my departure, a sense of solitude unexpectedly hits me. I'm alone on the trail for the first time. Without a hiking companion, I'm fully aware of every aspect of my surroundings.

What's that noise?

Another squirrel.

OK, Derick, just enjoy the trail. It's safe out here, fool, I tell myself.

I decide to focus on my poles.

Left pole forward, right leg forward. Right pole forward, left leg forward. I think I got it . . .

I nearly trip over my left pole.

By lunchtime, I'm still clueless about how to use my poles and I'm in need of a bathroom, but of course there is no bathroom out here.

A privy—that's what it's called.

I follow blue blazes down a side trail that leads me to Stover Creek Shelter.

I set my bag on a picnic table and follow the sign to the privy. I find it but then realize I forgot my toilet paper and hand sanitizer, so I rush back to retrieve them.

When I return to the privy, I stand and stare at it for a moment. Not once in my entire life has a situation forced me to poop outside, but I now have to bare my butt cheeks over a hole? Inside, wooden walls surround me, but there isn't a door, and the walls are only about 5 feet high. Wooden poles in the corners hold up a roof several feet higher than the wall. It's great ventilation, and I can almost sit and enjoy the scenery. But it does little to ease my mind about being exposed to whomever may stroll in. I realize the word *privy* must derive from the word *privacy,* something I definitely don't feel at the moment.

I drop my pants and hover over a hole that is dressed with a toilet seat. I lean back and brace myself against the back wall. Feeling vulnerable, I stare at the doorless entrance. The opening to the privy is facing away from the shelter and surrounding tentsites, which is what passes for privacy out here, I suppose. Is there some kind of privy etiquette I don't know about? Do I make some kind of noise so no one walks in on me?

I hurriedly finish and head back to the picnic table for my backpack. Before I leave, I decide to walk over to the shelter and check out the guest register. I dig the idea that hikers can leave entries about their hike thus far, their stay in the shelter, where they're headed, or whatever's on their mind. It's also a great way to see where others are along the trail. I look forward to reading some good stories and comments during my journey.

Five hikers sit at a picnic table in front of the shelter, seemingly in no hurry to start their day of hiking. I greet them, grab the register, and join them at the table. I skim over the entries. Beside weather updates and comments about how nice this new shelter is, there are several entries about the approach trail steps. The overall consensus is that it ain't easy, which makes me feel better about my degree of fitness. As I set out for Hawk Mountain Shelter, I'm imagining that the approach trail will make the rest of my hike seem easy by comparison.

I get to Hawk Mountain Shelter a little before 2 P.M., hoping to see my three amigos. They're not here, but I read in the register that they did stop here for lunch and are moving on to find a campsite nearby.

Am I done for the day, or do I try to catch up with them?

I've hiked about 8 miles to this shelter. The plan was to average 8 miles on my first few days. I'm not yet sure what I'm able to do, and I don't want to push myself to the point of injury. I'm in for at least five months. I decide to stick to my plan.

Well, I'm sure I'll see my three friends again.

I must be dehydrated because I'm not thinking straight. Searching for a water source, I take a wrong trail in my flip-flops and get lost for 40 minutes.

Now it's 5 P.M., all the campsites are taken, and the shelter is filled with hikers. A hiker named Doug and a few other guys are playing a game of Wiffle ball by the shelter. My exhaustion from the water debacle keeps me from joining the fun. But before I call it a night, I find enough strength to lift a pen and write a few words in my journal.

White blazes aren't the only markers to follow . . . there are blue ones too. They lead to privies and water sources. Stick to these markers! Aimlessly wandering into unmarked woods is a thick-headed move.

My pen stops writing as I take a moment to form a productive thought about the day. I finally write: *Dude, just follow the blazes!*

CHAPTER 5

Why the AT?

THE SOUND OF UNZIPPING TENTS AND BACKPACKS DROWNS OUT WHAT I expected would be another morning filled with nature's harmonious music. Instead of singing birds, I hear eager hikers emerging from their tents, ready to tackle another day of AT hiking. I myself am eager to do nothing but bury my head deeper into my sleeping bag. I want to spend more time wrapped in comfort before I even *think* about freeing myself from its cozy embrace. Once again, I'm going to be the last one to leave camp—and frankly, I'm cool with that. It's 7:30 A.M., and if I was in NYC, I would still be under my bedcovers, in the midst of a third or fourth dream, hours away from stirring awake. After years of being a night owl in the big city, this early morning routine is going to take some getting used to.

By 10 A.M.—late for a hiker, but still early for this New Yorker—I finish my cup of instant coffee and do a quick stretch.

"Hey, how are ya? Are you thru-hiking?" I hear as I start toward the white-blazed trail.

Walking in my direction is a friendly-looking guy who greets me with a big smile and even bigger energy.

"Hey. Yeah, what about you?" I reply.

"I sure am! I'm here with my dad. Hiking the dream! I'm Chris," he says with an extraordinary amount of glee. He seems to bounce when he speaks, as if every word tickles his insides as they come out. I immediately like him.

"Did you guys stay here last night? I thought I was the last one leaving this morning," I say.

"Nah, we stayed at a campsite near Three Forks, about 4 miles south of here. We just stopped in for a break."

"You guys already did 4 miles? Jeez, I haven't even started," I say.

"That's OK. You're here hiking the Appalachian Trail! That's what truly matters. Hike your own hike," he says.

"True indeed," I respond.

Why is this guy so perky? My curiosity makes me don a trench coat and pick up my pipe and magnifying glass. I want to find out why Happy Feet here looks ready to jump out of his skin and do a dance in honor of the AT gods.

"Any idea how far you guys are going today?" I ask while I try to figure out his angle.

"I'm not sure. I have to see how my dad feels," he says.

Hmm. He could just be a good guy. Although he talks with unusual fervor, there's nothing else out of the ordinary. Still, a part of me wonders if I just met the solution to world peace. I want to stay and talk more to this guy, but I also feel a need to finally start hiking.

"Well, I hope I see you guys on the trail," I say.

"Yeah, see ya," he says as he bounces to the shelter like Tigger from *Winnie the Pooh*.

Wow, that dude is super jolly. Either his exuberance is genuine or he gets help from some happy pills—or maybe a little of both. I'll go with the latter explanation for now.

It's a cloudy but overall pleasant day for a hike. The air is refreshing, and occasionally a cool breeze passes through the bare trees, softly blowing on my skin. For the first time, I feel calm and comfortable hiking in the woods. I smile. Moments like this are why I left the city. No burdens, no worries, just me and nature—and the many hikers I now begin to pass on the trail.

Dang, Grand Central station is less busy.

I'm not the lone drifter of yesterday. In fact, by the time I reach Gooch Mountain Shelter, at around 2 o'clock, I have passed nineteen hikers.

After reading in the shelter log that my three elusive friends are camping 8.5 miles away, I abandon the notion that I will see them again. They are moving way too fast.

Well, fellas, it was nice knowing ya.

I walk down one of three short trails that lead to a camp area. I pass a tent already pitched, housing a sleeping hiker. Just past that tent, there's a large open area, but I decide on a smaller site near a tree with low, outstretched branches. I sit down on a log outside my tent to relax and take in my surroundings.

Soon more hikers arrive, seeking free ground to pitch their tents.

"Look, Derick's here!" someone says. "I thought you would've reached Blood Mountain by now."

I turn to see Chris, the overly enthusiastic hiker I met at Hawk Mountain Shelter, with an older hiker I'm guessing is his dad. I greet them.

"Dude, you must have been moving at the speed of light, because I didn't see you after Hawk Mountain Shelter," he says with such ebullience that I fight back a titter.

"It was a perfect day for a hike, and I was feeling energetic," I say. "I guess I was moving faster than I thought. I got here about an hour ago."

I didn't expect to stop this early, but I'm still adjusting to all-day hiking with a heavy pack, so pushing myself doesn't make sense. Chris introduces his dad as Downhill, a trail name just given to him because he loves hiking down hills and mountains.

"Hello, Downhill. No trail name yet for me," I say.

"We'll have to work on that," Chris replies.

I'm sure he'll make it a jubilant one.

"Yeah, we'll find one for you too," I respond.

"Gravity Master was suggested, since I'm flying over these mountains," he says with a pride that's not the least bit arrogant.

"I still think you should go with High Gear or Overdrive," his dad chimes in.

"Well, I'll see which one sticks," he responds.

I want to say, *What about Tigger?* But instead I say, "You should take a name that you like. You'll be stuck with it for a while."

The area around me quickly begins to fill up with tents. Chris and his dad settle into the campsite next to mine. I gaze around at what looks and feels like the beginnings of a community. I hear people greet each other as they perform their rounds, making acquaintances, sharing experiences, and speculating about what's to come. There are so many eager bodies bursting with the hope of journeying all the way to Maine. At this point in the game, everyone is in first place, but being first is not the goal in this sport; it's about reaching the final destination.

"Man, you're really using that tree," I hear someone say.

I turn to see a giant dressed in hiking clothes. He glances over my clothes, camp towel, Platypus, and bandana hanging on low, outstretched branches.

"Yeah, it's Mother Nature's clothesline."

"You mind if I join you?" he asks. Not waiting for my answer, he sits on the ground and sets a small gas stove in front of him.

"Not at all, the more the merrier," I say, glad to have the company.

He gets settled and introduces himself as Rich.

"What are you using to heat up your food?" I ask, curious if it's a stove I should have gone with.

"A Jetboil. It uses these isobutane canisters. Is that an alcohol stove?" he asks, pointing at my mini stove.

"Yeah, it's the lightest one I could find," I explain.

"You like it?"

"So far, yeah. It heats up my food and boils water for coffee. That's all I ask."

We hear a pop as he starts his Jetboil.

"I haven't figured out why it does that," he says with a smile.

"Yeah, that didn't sound right. Hope you don't blow us both up," I say half-jokingly, edging away from the stove.

He looks at his potentially perilous Jetboil stove. "You gotta love it," he says.

I dig this guy's attitude.

"So, what's your story? What do you do that you're able to be homeless for several months?" he asks.

I realize that in a way, I am homeless.

"Well, I suppose it was a series of lucky breaks," I start. "I just returned from a trip to Italy, and I have time to spare before I embark on the next responsible stage of my life."

"Cool. Why the AT?" he asks.

I contemplate the question, one that I expect I'll be asked several more times on this journey.

"Well, a friend of mine recommended *A Walk in the Woods*, a funny book by Bill Bryson," I start.

"Yeah, I read it."

"Well, up to that point I'd never heard of the Appalachian Trail, but after reading his book, the thought of hiking it stuck with me. I kept thinking, *How would I fare?* That question became a driving force. So when I found myself with the time and the resources, I had no good reason not to do it."

"Great, man," he says with a wide smile.

"What about you?" I ask. "Why are you doing the AT?"

"To get away from the wife," he quickly responds and then lets out a loud, heavy laugh.

"Nah, I have wanted to do the AT ever since my uncle attempted it back in the 1960s. He made it 120 miles but then had issues with head lice or something like that. He lost interest after that, but my interest was just beginning. I never let go of the idea."

"How does your wife feel about you leaving her for half a year?"

"Well, she's not thrilled about it," he says with a boisterous laugh. "Look, I'm 52 years old. I've wanted to do this for a long time. She at least gets that."

I get it as well, and with that, Rich finishes his meal and retires into his tent.

At that moment I hear Downhill speaking to his son, as they sit outside their tent. "You would know better than me," he says.

"Where exactly is the pain?" Chris asks his father.

"Just below my kneecap," Downhill replies, touching that part of his leg.

"Well, you've had that issue for months. There's not much that can be done, that I know of. Any doctor will tell you the best solution is to stay off your feet and elevate your leg, but that's not an option out here, is it Pop?"

Chris's shirt is off, revealing a well-defined chest. His calves have not been neglected either, and I'm sure he lifts weights. This guy looks like a typical jock but sounds like a doctor. This happy-go-lucky bodybuilder with brains continues to pique my curiosity.

As I put away my mini stove and seal my food bag, I continue listening to Chris and Downhill's conversation. They seem to welcome an audience, so it doesn't feel as if I'm eavesdropping. I get a sense that they enjoy making a show of their father-son relationship—a show I find somewhat comical.

"Hey, Pop, why is your tent so close to mine? When it gets dark, I'm going to trip over your tent fly," Chris says.

"I thought you wanted us to get closer out here, you know, bond?" Downhill replies, grinning at his quip.

"Yeah, but not like that. What's wrong with you, old man?" Chris says with playful irritation.

The scene is endearing . . . in a macho man way.

Chris notices my amusement and asks, "How's it going?" as his dad heads into the trees behind our campsite.

"I'm good. How are you guys?"

"Oh, we're great. Dad likes to mess with me. I can't believe we're hiking the Appalachian Trail!" he says with full-on Tigger zeal.

"Yeah, I know. A little spontaneous planning, and now I'm actually here. It's great that you're hiking with your dad," I say.

"We hike together a lot. We did the Smokies last year going southbound."

"That's cool. I'm looking forward to the Smokies. Actually, this whole trip is all new to me, so I'm looking forward to every day out here," I say, taking on some of Chris's spirited demeanor.

"Where are you from?"

"New York City."

"Wow, not many hiking trails or campsites there."

"Nah. This is all surreal for me. The first time I slept in a tent was at Springer Mountain. I've done a day hike, but that was in Italy, and . . . well, the Italians have their special way of hiking. When we got to the top of the mountain, we had a big lunch with lots of wine. Needless to say, I don't remember how I got back down. So, other than that little stint, I've done zero hiking, no long-distance, and no camping."

"Really?" he asks with astonishment.

I got the same reaction from Josh, Mike, and Swiss on my first night at Springer Mountain. It didn't cross my mind that what I'm doing is out of the ordinary.

"I know it may sound a little ambitious for me to go right into a thru-hike without at least one overnight hike," I say, "but I'm sure I'm not the first or the last person to do such a thing. Live life, right?"

Hearing myself say this out loud makes me aware of how extreme this choice really is. A twinge of nervous pain hits my stomach.

"That's incredible. The hardest step is getting out here . . . and you've done that. I know you'll make it all the way. I have a good feeling about you." He says it with such certainty that if he said I could fly to Maine, I would start flapping my arms.

My admitting that I'm attempting a thru-hike, having never hiked or camped before, probably would leave most people feeling uncertain of my success, but not Chris. If I had any reservations about making it to Katahdin, he just magically poofed them away.

"Did you have to quit your job to do the AT?" I ask, searching for answers to satisfy my curiosity about this unusually cheerful person.

"I'm a pharmacist," he says.

Aha, he's a druggist! That's how he gets his happy! I knew it wasn't natural. Yet he doesn't have the look of someone hooked on pills.

"I gave my notice at the pharmacy. They were OK with my decision and said I could return after my thru-hike."

I fire a few more questions until my inquisitiveness is satisfied. Every answer he gives is conveyed with a boost of joy, something I've never seen before.

It's my third day out here, and I've already met so many different types of people. I'm amazed that, thus far, I've felt a connection with them all. Sure, we have thru-hiking in common, but there's more to it than that.

Why the AT?

I know I'll get that question from many people, but with all of this splendid socializing with good-natured hikers, the real question in my mind at this point is, *Why not the AT?*

CHAPTER 6

Farewell to Indoor Plumbing

"DID YOU JUST WASH UP?" I ASK DOWNHILL AS HE EMERGES FROM THE woods behind our campsite.

I've gone four days without a shower . . . *four sweaty, hiking, funky days.* That, for sure, was not part of my AT plan. This is the longest I've gone without a proper shower since—shoot, unless Mother didn't bathe her infant child, I don't think I've ever gone this long unbathed. Although I've rinsed myself off at streams and used body wipes, I reek of something awful. Stenchy cheese smells floral compared to me. At no time in my life have I ever smelled anything like what is emitting from my body at this moment. This goes against all of my fastidious hygiene habits.

Some people are perfectly OK with being grungy on a backpacking trip or even in their daily lives. I'm just not one of those people.

"I did," Downhill replies, sounding refreshed.

"Where did you go?" I ask.

I have wanted to try my outdoor pocket shower since I started the trail, but I've been too tired or too busy getting lost. This is the first real opportunity I've had. "I just walked through the trees back there, far enough that no one could see me," he says pointing over his shoulder.

"Well, that's where I'm headed," I say. "I need to destinkify myself."

I smell like roadkill that was taken out of a dumpster and left in the back of a busted refrigerator.

"I bet the armpits of the homeless guy on the A train smell sweeter than mine," I add, lifting my arm for a sniff.

That comment probably makes sense only to me, unless Downhill and his son have ever entered a New York City subway car only to have the fetor of something awful punch them right in the nose.

After filling my pocket shower with water from the spring, I make my way toward the trees behind our campsite. The ground begins to slope downward, and the farther I get from camp, the steeper the grade gets. With flip-flops on, it's difficult not to slip on the dry leaves or trip over fallen branches. Dirt begins to coat my toes, and I wonder how I'll keep them clean while climbing back.

After a few more yards I stop, not trusting myself to go any farther without getting lost. The last thing I want is to stray too far from camp with nearly nothing on, and only soap and a camp towel for survival tools. I look up for a branch strong enough to hang my pocket shower on. The shower's instructions are printed on its small carrying case: Use at least 100 meters from any water source. Well, I'm on the side of a mountain, and the spring is on the other side of camp.

Check.

The instructions also say I should use only biodegradable soap. That one I knew already.

So, again, check.

I toss the thin nylon rope tied to the top of the pocket shower over a branch that looks sturdy enough to support 10 liters of water. I pull the bag up just above my shoulders and wrap the rope around the tree. I take off my T-shirt and shorts. I grab my Dr. Bronner's all-purpose, environmentally friendly camp soap. I use this soap to bathe, to wash my clothes, to clean my gear, and—if necessary—to brush my teeth.

I squeeze some of the soap into my hand then—*hey!*

I slip but manage to catch the tree the shower is hanging on. I find my balance briefly before slipping again. I'm going to have to hone my physical abilities if I plan on showering upright. Meanwhile, my right foot slips right out of my flip-flop.

Damn it! I need the balance and coordination of an Olympic gymnast to keep from falling off this mountain.

I lean on the tree with one hand, and with the other I start lathering myself. A breeze chills the air, sending goose bumps across my body. The cold water makes me squeal.

I better make a quick job of this.

I let go of the tree and balance myself as I wash off the soap. I slip again on some leaves, and a few stick to my legs. I catch the side of the tree, but then I lose my grip and fall face first. The dry leaves soften my landing, but my head bounces as I slip farther downhill. A force—yes, OK, gravity—seems to be pulling me down the mountainside. I grasp for roots but come up with handfuls of broken branches. I continue to slide, my gymnast skills failing me horribly. I must look like an Alpine skier who has miscalculated a turn and is flying out of control. Dried leaves find their way into my mouth. My hair is decorated with forest, a fern now sits on my head. My entire wet body is covered in dirt, leaves, and twigs. I feel like I've been tarred and feathered. If I wasn't so astounded, I would cry with laughter.

"Son of a birch tree! What just happened?" I demand.

I look back up at where I should be showering instead of lying here, several yards below, buried under layers of undergrowth and looking like a herbaceous Yeti. I've never wanted to wash myself more than I do at this moment. I slowly work my way back to my hanging shower. I lean my shoulder on the tree and stare at this crappy gadget I felt the need to have. I wipe what detritus I can off my body, lather once more, and wash off the soap.

Fff—for the love of forest! It is cold! Still, I'd better get used to bathing outside, "because smelling like butt is not an option for me," I adamantly say out loud.

I carefully climb back toward my tent, feeling more fatigued from the shower than from today's hike. I'm ready for a good night's sleep.

I can't sleep. Not until I go outside and pee. I've been holding it for 40 minutes. Last night I held it in, relieving myself outside only when daylight arrived and I felt safe. But it's not even midnight. It's pitch dark out there, and I have to go really bad.

Come on. I'm going to have to do it eventually. What do I think will happen? It's perfectly safe out there. Isn't that what I told everyone in New York? Derick, just go already!

After an hour of talking myself into it, I work up the courage to strap on my headlamp and zip open my tent.

Man, tent zippers are loud. I'm going to wake everyone up.

I step out and scan the dark trees, waiting for movement.

OK, the coast is clear. Now, where do I go? Too many tents around. Someone will hear me. I'll have to walk away from the campsite. Damn. OK, OK, OK. Here I go.

That's cool—reflective strips on the tent fabric shine as I pass with my headlamp. I'm glad to see there's no way I could trip over a tent. I'd hate to crash on top of one, frightening a sleeping hiker or, worse yet, destroying someone's portable home.

I find a blue blaze and decide to walk toward the privy. Eyes wide, I sweep my head around, shining a beam of light 10 feet in front of me, searching for a place to pee. At that moment, coming out of the darkness and entering the far end of my ray of light, something flies right at me.

What is that? Oh!

A moth is cruising toward me at the speed of light, and this creature of the night is not slowing down.

What is it trying to—?

BAM!

It plows directly into my face, its wings flapping violently against my eyelashes. "What the hell!" I screech, abandoning any concern I had for the sleeping hikers around me.

I swat at the moth but miss, instead smacking myself in the eye and knocking my headlamp to the side of my face. I stagger, bracing myself against a tree. Is this what I get for leaving the safety of my tent in the middle of the night?

Attacked! I was attacked by mother-flying Mothra!

I straighten my lamp and quickly finding the nearest tree to do what I came out here for in the first place.

This peeing at night thing is nothing but trouble. I'd better head back to my tent before something bigger and more dangerous joins the assault. With one useful eye and the other still irritated by the smite, I hurry back to my tent, tripping, stumbling, and nearly falling over a tree root.

Curses. Nature should put reflector strips on those too.

It's hazardous, roaming out here in the dark. Is this how it's always going to be? I'm not sure I'll ever truly feel at ease without indoor plumbing, but I'll have to endure. Funny how you don't really appreciate something until it disappears from your life.

CHAPTER 7

A Machete Would Have Been Better

"WHY WOULD YOU WANT TO TENT THERE?" I HEAR A SURLY VOICE ASK.

I turn to see thick, black-framed glasses perched on a long face that's sticking out of a tent a yard away from me. All of the tentsites at Lance Creek are taken, so I have no choice but to claim a less favorable spot mere inches from the trail.

It's been a long, grueling day. I left camp this morning hours after the other hikers. It's been raining off and on all day. I hiked with pain running from my shoulder to my neck. I just want to stop and rest. Yeah, I'll settle for this crummy patch of earth for the night.

"Well, the tent platforms down there are all taken," I reply, pointing at a long line of tents.

The AT goes up a small ascent to the right, and just past the start of that climb are platforms filled with tents.

"What about over there?" With his head, he indicates a larger clearing across the trail, farther from his tent.

"Well, there's still two other hikers arriving, and they could use a bigger spot, so I thought I'd leave it for them," I reply.

Earlier in the day I met Sonja and her friend Eva who both came all the way from Germany to hike the AT.

"Hmph," he snorts and then retracts his head into his tent.

His food bag hangs on a low branch nearby, only a few feet off the ground. An attached cord runs into his tent.

I don't get it. I thought the purpose of hanging a food bag was to keep it out of the reach of animals. What's he going to do when that cord alerts him of a hungry bear—wrestle it? What if a bear *does* come sniffing around? My tent is right near his. I certainly don't want to be a casualty of this guy's weak bear hangin' skills. Before I say something, I'll give him some time to prove he's not exceedingly clueless.

I turn away and secure my tent fly, toss my backpack in my tent, and jump in after it. It's not fun pitching a tent in the rain. I resolve to wait until it stops before I stroll over to the campsite to find Rich, Chris, and Downhill. After my encounter with Mr.-Get-Off-My-Property-or-I'll-Shoot, I'm looking forward to some friendly faces.

It doesn't take long for the rain to stop. I step out of my tent and look over at the crowded campsite.

"Are you happy with your tent?"

My new neighbor's head, once again, is sticking out of his tent. This is possibly an attempt on his part at making conversation. Still, I'm not convinced. His voice sounds more critical than curious. I answer in as friendly a manner as I can manage: "It's the first tent I've ever owned, so I can't make any comparisons. But yeah, I'm happy. It keeps me dry and warm."

"Looks pretty small," he replies, his words again sounding more like a knock than an observation.

In an effort to be cordial, I ask him if he's thru-hiking.

"No, I'm just going north," he replies vaguely.

"Oh, OK," I say, turning my attention to the laughter coming from the crowd of tents. "Looks like they're having fun."

"The group last night was loud. They were up late drinking and playing the harmonica. They make you guys look like wimps," he declares. "Guess that's not a bad thing," he quietly adds to himself.

Baffled, I ignore the comment. *This guy is strange.*

I resolve to keep it cool so as not to spark any crazy impulses he may have. I sincerely do not wish to end up in an Alfred Hitchcock movie. Or even worse, a B movie with a name like *Terror on the Trail*, in which a guy in a hockey mask chops me into little pieces which he then hangs in a bag just low enough for the bears to reach, distracting them from going for his own food bag hanging over his tent.

"So, you did a zero today?" I ask.

"I'm not hiking in this rain," he says with a grumble before he pops his head back into his cave-tent.

What kind of Neanderthal response is that?

This is my fourth day on the trail, and thus far I've had nothing but friendly encounters. Even on a rainy day like today, I saw many smiles and exchanged pleasantries with wet and tired hikers. But this guy is different: He's either a psychopath or has zero social skills. I'll give him the benefit of the doubt and say he's just socially inept. If he were a serial killer, he'd have a better personality and would have me completely under his spell right now. You know how charming those guys are.

When the rain stops, I take advantage of the dry spell to visit the hikers at the campground. I follow the trail for a few yards then veer to the right, where I see Rich talking to Downhill. Rich is wearing a T-shirt tucked into black long underwear pulled up way past his waist. The sight is nearly too much for me. It takes all the will I can muster not to burst out laughing.

How did he ever find underwear to fit his tall frame?

Rich calls out to me. "Look who decided to join the party! Thought you would've caught up with me on the trail. I tried to save you a spot, but it got crowded fast. All that's left is this small area covered in roots."

I try not to give his lower attire any attention for fear I may lose my composure.

Feeling a smile take over my face, I say, "I was having some trouble with my backpack and my shoulder—they weren't getting along. My backpack was kicking my shoulder's butt, so I had to stop and separate them a few times."

I rub my left shoulder.

"You'll figure it out," Rich says. "We were just talking about getting a cabin at Neels Gap—you, me, Downhill, and Chris. It'll be cheaper with four of us. We can dry off and do laundry."

"And take a shower?" I ask enthusiastically.

"Yeah, and there's a kitchen and a couple of bedrooms," Rich says.

"You had me at shower," I say, giddy at the thought.

I shudder to think about how I must smell right now. I wonder if it might be an effective serial killer repellent.

I hang with the guys a while before it starts to rain again. As I run back to my tent, I see two hikers approaching.

"Hi, Sonja and Eva. All the tent platforms are taken, but there's a big enough area for both of you right here," I say, gesturing at the spot across the trail from my tent.

"Oh, thanks," Sonja says.

They both look tired, so I excuse myself, giving them time to set up camp and finish their day. I crawl into my tent to read until the rain stops again. I hear the new arrivals conversing in German while they hurriedly pitch their tents in the rain.

"Hey," I hear our suspicious neighbor say to the girls as they get themselves settled.

"Hey," they both reply.

"Do you speak English?" he asks.

He clearly heard me talking to the girls when they arrived, so this must be another awkward attempt on his part at making conversation. If this guy is bucking for the position of homeowners' association president, he'd better brush up on his social skills, because he's not getting my vote.

"Yeah, do you?" I hear Sonja shoot back.

I like this girl—she's sassy.

"Yeah. What are your names?" he asks. His tone is much more congenial than when he spoke to me. He now sounds like a teenage boy fumbling his words in an awkward effort to ask a girl out.

"I'm Sonja, and this is Eva. You?"

"I'm Jason," he says.

Jason? We got Friday the 13th *up in here!*

I think back to a conversation I had with my brother. He wanted me to strap a small machete to my chest for this hike. I can hear him now: *"I told you, fool!"*

OK, I need to calm down and stop being paranoid.

The rain passes as the women finish pitching their tents. I'm getting antsy and eager to join in a conversation. Once more, I walk toward camp, anticipating a nice relaxing dialogue with some normal people—people who do not want to murder me in my sleep. I meet two new hikers, Nora and her brother Matthew, who are hiking together for three weeks. Nora is doing a thru-hike, but Matthew decided to join her for the first leg because he didn't like the idea of her going it alone. I get the feeling Nora would have liked him to accompany her later, after she had some time on the trail by herself.

I also talk with Jolly 3-0, a hiker I've seen before on the trail. His trail name comes from the call sign of a rescue helicopter he was flying during what turned out to be the most successful airborne rescue mission in the Vietnam War. I dig that, and it's one of my favorite trail name stories so far.

Rich, as it turns out, started his thru-hike with the trail name Big Foot. I'm not surprised. Six foot eight, with two different-size feet—one is 13.5, the other 15. Add the high-wearing, wedgie-makin' underwear, and you have what amounts to an oddity, a missing link, but also an endearing guy with a contagious laugh.

L-Dog, Kim, and Dark Age, who have dubbed themselves the Asylum Train, are the last of the hikers to trickle into camp. L-Dog greets us with a smile and positive words about the wet day. "Embrace the rain," he announces.

"—and quickly hike between raindrops," I add. I dance around, miming an attempt to avoid raindrops in an effort to inject the situation with silliness.

Kim has taken L-Dog's words of encouragement to heart and finished her day with a big smile and a friendly attitude, but Dark Age is a sorry sight. A lock of wet hair is stuck to the side of his face. He looks like someone who has suffered a grave injustice and now lives only for retribution. In reply to my greeting, without slowing his pace, he gives me a hard stare and a grunt.

Is this the same guy that was so gung-ho about the AT mere days ago? I guess the rain changed that. He's definitely not embracing it.

Feeling hungry, I head back to my tent. To my surprise, the social delinquent is out of his tent, standing next to Eva. This is my first full view of him. He's tall, lean, and appears to have the strength to abduct a young German woman. He looks down at Eva as she skims through an AT guide that he seems to have shared with her. She hands it back to him, thanks him, and quickly crosses back to the side of the trail where her tent is. I sense an uneasiness from Eva, which makes me nervous. *So it's not my imagination!*

During my visit with the other hikers, I discovered there are a few more tentsites past the tent platforms. I'm tempted to gather my gear and get far away from Friday the 13th, but I don't want to leave Sonja and Eva to fend for themselves. Plus, I'm too hungry to pack up and leave.

After eating and watching Big Foot hang our food bags together, I see the sun is beginning to go down. Unlike vampires, the first sign of darkness causes hikers to scatter into their tents. Peaceful silence blankets our camp. Then I hear my odd neighbor making noises that sound like he's trying to start a fire by striking a flint.

Shingt, shingt, shingt . . .

"Damn!" he cries out, oblivious to how disturbing he is being.

Earlier Sonja asked Jason to hang his food bag somewhere else, away from our camping area. Since then, the girls have been silent, so I assume they are trying to sleep. But curses and the sound of steel on flint are far from a lullaby.

"Trying to get that lit, I see," I hear someone ask Jason while passing his tent on the way to the water source.

Don't go there! I want to warn the passerby.

"Yeah. I'm ready to kill somebody," says Jason Voorhees.

Damn! I didn't need to hear that.

I want to pack everything and find that root-filled spot I saw next to Big Foot's tent. It'll be uncomfortable, but it's better than being murdered.

Man, oh man . . . I can't leave the girls here alone with him.

I'm not sure if he just doesn't like me near him or if he *really* likes the women near him. Either way, the three of us are a target. Should I at least tell Rich or Chris, just in case I go missing?

I search my backpack and find my multitool, which has a 1.5-inch knife.

Like I'm expected to defend myself with this? You were right, brother—a machete would have been better.

Well, this Fisher-Price toy knife, which looks like it would tickle him instead of doing serious harm, is all I have. I'll do whatever I need to do to stay alive, even if I have to be on guard all night.

I fall asleep instantly. The next thing I know, it's morning. My utility knife is still clutched in my hand. I wake from a dream in which my brother is duct-taping a machete to my chest—and realize that I will live to hike another day.

CHAPTER 8

Rain, Pain & Zombie Hiking

I WAKE TO THE SOUND OF TENTS, BACKPACKS, AND SLEEPING BAGS BEING zipped, unzipped, and zipped again. There's no need to set an alarm out here, because once daylight breaks, the morning air is filled with the sound of zippers. It was just a few days ago that chirping birds roused me from a deep sleep. Now it feels as if that was just a dream.

Then it occurs to me . . .

I'm still alive! Jason didn't—but wait . . . the girls!

I unzip my tent and poke my head out. I look over at where Sonja and Eva camped. I remain still, my eyes fixed on their tents, my ears seeking sounds of movement. I look at Jason's tent and hear nothing. I direct my attention back to the women, and finally, after what feels like an eternity, I hear them stirring. I must have been holding my breath, because I let out such a powerful exhale that I almost fall backward.

The women are safe, and I can hear them conversing in German. It's a lovely language. Why did I ever think it sounded harsh or angry?

"Here's your food bag," Sonja says from outside my tent.

I'm spooked, especially because I was just thinking about them. It's as if she came over to say, "Hey, stop thinking about us, perv!"

I want to say, "No, it's not like that. I was . . . " but I quickly recover and unzip my tent. She places my food bag on the ground by my tent and greets me with, "Good morning," and a smile.

"Thanks," I mutter.

Big Foot arrives to suggest that we hike together this morning. I'm finishing my breakfast when he returns a few minutes later to see how far I've gotten in terms of hiking *today*.

"I'm slow at the start. I'll speed it up, or I can catch up with you on the trail," I say, hoping I don't need to move any faster than I already am.

Besides, it's drizzling, and I don't move fast in the rain. Actually, I don't move fast in the early morning, period.

He shrugs, then says, "Nah, I'll wait for you."

"OK," I respond, but part of me hoped he would go on ahead without me.

Big Foot strolls back as I'm unhooking my tent poles.

"Ready yet?" he says with a smile.

"Almost," I respond, now feeling rushed.

He greets Sonja and Eva, who are just finishing their breakfast.

Looks like I'm not going to be the last person leaving camp. There's a first time for everything.

Big Foot must be feeling pressed for time, because he starts to unhook my tent poles. Apparently I'm not moving fast enough for him. I leave him to it as I proceed to fold my tent fly, and within minutes we're ready to go. We wish Sonja and Eva happy trails as we head to Neels Gap. There we plan to share a cabin with Downhill and his son Chris, who has gone ahead to secure the cabin for the four of us.

"Lead the way, Derick. You're probably faster than I am," Big Foot says.

"I'm not sure about that. Climbs are my Achilles' heel."

Even as a runner, I've found ascents difficult. I lose my stamina within seconds of any elevation gain. Hiking up Blood Mountain, the highest peak in the Georgia section of the Appalachian Trail, will not be easy for me. Then there's the issue of my sore shoulder; the pain I felt yesterday was excruciating. I changed the way I wear my backpack on my body this morning, but I'm not sure if it will ease the pressure off my shoulder. Still, I begin with high hopes for a pain-free day.

Raindrops land with a light spatter on the leaves, the sound similar to soft clapping hands. The noise diverts my mind from the shoulder pain that started about an hour into our hike. I try losing myself in the peaceful aura and gentle patter of falling rain. I think of how I could be at home in New York City—dry, warm, lying comfortably in bed.

Rain is part of this adventure. I can't change that, but I can prepare for it. I don a rain jacket that has a hood large enough to cover my long hair. I also have a rain cover for my backpack and gaiters to prevent my socks from getting wet. But the most essential tool that I have is *acceptance*. Rain will be part of my thru-hike, no matter what. I will have to trek through areas that may have significant snowfall early in spring and endure thunderstorms that can hit with little warning. This journey will go better if I don't dread and curse the things I cannot control.

So come on, rain, and do what you do. I'll do what I came here to do, and perhaps we'll get along.

I stop and pull off my pack. Big Foot sees the pain I'm in and asks if I'm OK.

"I'm not sure . . . I have to stop . . . my shoulder . . . I tried readjusting my straps on my pack, but it doesn't seem to be helping."

"Yeah, you look like a zombie lumbering up the trail. It's entertaining," he says, laughing.

"Hey, I aim to please," I respond.

The rain cuts our break short, forcing us to start moving again.

Minutes later, I say, "Listen Big Foot, my shoulder is slowing me down. You'd better go on ahead of me." I try not to show how much pain I'm in.

He agrees to move on and meet me at the shelter for lunch.

A zombie lumbering up the trail . . . yeah, that's what I feel like: the hiking dead. I watch my new friend plod up the mountain. His pace steady, he looks like a colossus with a backpack. His tall form, heavy footsteps, and long strides remind me of a construction crane controlled by a skilled yet cautious operator. He works fast enough to get the job done but never haphazardly.

After taking only a few steps, I stop once again and slip my pack off. Rubbing my left shoulder, I wonder how I'll make it to Maine with this sharp pain tearing through my shoulder. I've taken my backpack off three times in only 30 minutes. I'm obviously wearing this pack wrong, but I have no idea how to fix the problem.

The rain continues to come down, adding to my discomfort. I try to focus on the raindrops, listening to the noise they make as they hit my rain jacket. For a moment the sound draws my mind away and I'm at peace. Then a cold stab rips up my neck. I hunch over in anguish, my eyes welling up. I welcome the warm tear that runs down my cheek—any sensation other than this pain.

I force myself up. I have to keep moving. I'll stop at Blood Mountain Shelter for rest and a meal break. Then I'll move on to Neels Gap, where hopefully someone can show me how to wear my backpack correctly.

Until then, I plod up steep Blood Mountain hunched over, with my pack resting on my right side. Finally the shelter summit appears. I feel like I just climbed a sacred mountain, and now this shelter is looking down at me, waiting to make my life better with blessings and answers to life's mysteries. As I get closer, though, it begins to look more like a small, broken-down cabin. I walk in and see a fireplace that I'm sure hasn't been used in a while. The room is empty, but I hear voices in an adjacent room. I feel a sharp pain as I take my pack off and drop it in a corner. I wonder if I'll make it down this mountain without wanting to scream in agony.

"Hello," I announce to the empty space.

"Over here, Derick," I hear.

I walk over and find Big Foot with a hiker named Brett. I drop to the floor next to them. Big Foot looks over at me.

"Are you OK?"

"Yeah, I just need to rest," I respond meekly, hanging my head between my legs.

Minutes later, Sonja and Eva join us. We all have lunch in this shelter/cabin that looks like it may have seen better days. While eating, I find out that Sonja's trail name is Soho, a merging of the first two letters of her first name and the first two letters of her last name, which begins with *Ho*. I won't even attempt to pronounce it for fear of how it may come out.

Eva's trail name is Halfway, which Big Foot gave her after he found out that she's only hiking to Harpers Ferry, the psychological halfway point of the AT. The actual halfway point is about 100 miles farther north, but I'm told that Harpers Ferry is a significant benchmark for thru-hikers and a great place to rest and prepare for the second half of an AT adventure.

With us is Brett, a young kid who at first reminded me of a farm boy. He's a strong-looking 19-year-old with a laugh like Disney's Goofy. He's soft-spoken, but I quickly find out that he's also funny and smart as a whip.

After lunch, we all head to Neels Gap. When we cross US Route 19, Chris is waiting with news that he was able to obtain a cabin for us. Big Foot and I go straight to Mountain Crossings outfitter, housed in an old stone interpretive center known as Walasi-Yi. There Big Foot asks one of the employees, an AT thru-hiker from a few years back, to sort through his backpack. The contents of his bag are spread out on the floor in a corner of the store. Big Foot sits cross-legged as he watches the staff member go over his pack with a masterful touch. As the man removes items, he explains why they're not needed. With the patience of a monk, he shows us how to get the optimum usage out of Big Foot's remaining gear. I'm impressed.

Done with Big Foot's backpack, he turns his attention to mine. He skillfully adjusts the straps and advises me to loosen all the straps every time I take my pack off. This will give me the best fit when I strap my pack back on. I'll try anything to stop this shoulder pain. If he tells me that carrying a chimpanzee will help, I'll run to the nearest monkey store to buy one.

"Also, let me show you something," he says, grabbing my trekking poles. "Run your hand under and through the strap, like this, and grab the handle. Now if your poles slip from your hands, you won't lose them." His demonstration leaves me in awe.

Filled with a sense of relief, I go over the day's final events in my head. I made it to Neels Gap, I'm in a cabin, and I'm able to wash up and rest for the night. I'm having dinner with my new hiker friends. I now know how to use and grip my poles. I've also learned how to wear my backpack correctly, hopefully relieving any pain I was causing myself. I knock on wood, cross my fingers, do a little prayer, and then a chant. I'll do anything short of an animal sacrifice to ensure myself of a pain-free hike tomorrow. Feeling assured, I now trust that I can hike like a normal being and not like a lifeless zombie.

Part 2

THE MOVING VILLAGE

CHAPTER 9

You're a Mr. Fabulous!

It's just past 9 a.m., and after a restful night's sleep at Blood Mountain Cabins in Neels Gap, Big Foot, Downhill, Chris, and I head out for an 8.5-mile hike to Low Gap Shelter. Although the four of us begin the day together, Chris and I find ourselves pulling ahead of Big Foot and Downhill. The two older hikers seem to have the same pace and are enjoying each other's company. Meanwhile Chris, feeling energetic as usual—especially now that his dad has a hiking buddy, so he doesn't need to worry about pulling too far ahead—is moving at a pace that I'm barely able to keep up with.

This guy is a torpedo with legs.

"I decided to take the trail name Overdrive," Chris announces, as if reading my mind. The name fits.

"Coolio, that is so you," I say. "Isn't that one of the names Downhill was suggesting for you?"

"Sure is. You're next," Chris, now Overdrive, announces.

"I'm sure one will present itself soon enough," I say. Although I sound unconcerned, I'm eager to receive a trail name.

As we continue to speed-hike, we converse about trail names. Overdrive suggests that a trail name should be bestowed on me by the end of the day, which suits me because I probably won't be 100 percent happy with whatever name I end up with. Reaching Maine and signing the shelter logs with *Derick (no trail name yet)* is a distinct possibility.

We reach a lookout point at Wildcat Mountain, which gives us a good reason to take our packs off. Except for some shoulder soreness, I'm pain free, thanks to the help I received at Mountain Crossings. The adjustments the staffer suggested made all the difference in the world.

By 2:30 P.M. we make it to Low Gap Shelter. It's crowded, but Overdrive and I find a flat enough spot with the ends of our tents nearly touching. Twenty minutes later, Big Foot arrives and finds a lumpy spot farther off by some fallen trees. Downhill decides to sleep in the shelter. Brett, now the Kid (named for his boyish looks), arrives with a tarp that he dumps on a patch of weeds and twigs.

Around 5:30 P.M., after everyone eats their dinner, Overdrive gathers a few hikers for a trail name brainstorming session. Joining the discussion is Nora, her brother Matt, Big Foot, the Kid, and Kevin, who are staying at the cabins as well.

We start with Nora's brother and quickly decide on Three Week since he's on the trail for only three weeks. Normally only thru-hikers get trail names, but *what the hey.*

Nora is next.

"OK, what are your hobbies? What's your favorite color? What's your favorite TV show?"

I'm hoping to get a laugh, but she perks up and says, "Actually, my favorite show is *Doctor Who*!"

"That settles it, your name is . . . TV Show. Next!"

"That's funny, but I don't think so," she says.

"What about Doctor Who?" Overdrive suggests.

"Too obvious, there's no story," she says, shooting down the suggestion.

Yeah, I can relate to not taking an obvious name.

"What about Who? It's vague enough to entice a story, right?" I add.

"Maybe . . . " she says, uncertain.

"I've never seen *Doctor Who*. Do you have a favorite character?" I ask.

"Yeah, Doctor Who," she says with a laugh.

"Well, what about Doc?" suggests Overdrive.

"That may work," she says shyly.

"It's Doc or TV Show—take it or leave it," I say.

This makes Big Foot laugh, sounding strangely like Herman Munster from the old black-and-white sitcom. He's a lovable, laughing giant who kind of moves like that character as well. His trail name should be Herman Munster.

Our attempt at finding Kevin a trail name is much more difficult.

"What's your sign?" I ask. "What's your favorite toothpaste? Boxers or briefs? That last question was for Nora's benefit. Getting nowhere, we decide to hold off on Kevin's nickname. It's my turn now.

Big Foot turns to me and says, "So, what's your sign? How many dreadlocks do you have? What's your favorite salsa move?" A burst of laughter erupts.

"Oh, you got jokes. Well, for your information, I'm down with the salsa move the *cucaracha*, and no, damn it, that will not be my name."

"Why don't you tell us a little about yourself?" Nora says.

"I thought you'd never ask."

I swing my arm with flair, as if unveiling one of the secret wonders of the world. "One day the universe decided to create a perfect being. It began with two brilliant stars for eyes, which were placed on a face that was deemed the most enchanting in the outer world. This being had flawless skin tone. Hair was harvested from a faraway planet where hair was equal to the highest form of holiness. To make him spicy, they added *sazon* and *adobo* seasoning and other mystical Spanish ingredients. When they were all finished—well, here I stand before you."

I fight back a creeping smile. Although they know that I'm kidding, my audience is hanging on every word.

"You're a hoot," says Kevin.

"I'm a what? That will not be my trail name," I say with a playful snap.

"The truth is that I've never done anything like this before"—I wave my arms, indicating our surroundings—"sleeping in a tent, hiking up mountains with a 40-pound backpack. My friends back home are shocked that I'm even doing this. I'm what you may call a metrosexual: I like to stay groomed, fresh, and well dressed."

The truth sounds as absurd as my first story.

"So, being out here without a shower in sight, well, it's out of character for me. I guess that's why I'm here . . . "

"You're a Mr. Fabulous!" Overdrive announces enthusiastically.

"Whaa—?" I begin.

"You're a Mr. Fabulous!" he repeats.

"If my friends back home knew that I was being called a Mr. Fabulous on the trail . . . well, I did joke that I wanted to figure out how to fit a full-length mirror into my backpack."

"You're definitely a Mr. Fabulous!" Overdrive proclaims once more.

"Isn't that the trumpet player from *The Blues Brothers*?" Big Foot asks.

"Yeah, he was well dressed and suave. You're definitely a Mr. Fabulous," Overdrive gleefully declares.

"How full of it will I sound? *Hi there, I'm Mr. Fabulous. What's your pleasure? Oh, yeah,*" I say with the deepest, most sensual voice I can muster. "That would be so creepy."

"Yeah, if you say it like that," Overdrive says with a laugh.

"I kind of like it," Nora says, with a playful flirt.

"Then I'll take it. You don't think it's too *all this is hotness* like?" I say, waving my open hand across my body as I move my hips from side to side.

"Not really. Once they meet you and see you've got a great personality, they'll realize that it's perfect," Overdrive says.

This guy is awesome. I'll have to keep him around as the captain of my cheerleading squad. He makes a brotha feel good about himself.

"Well," I say, "I guess I can try it. It'll be fun to see people's reactions. All right, Mr. Fabulous it is."

Mr. Fabulous? If I tell my friends in New York about this, they will certainly say that I persuaded others to call me by such a name.

With the trail name meeting complete, we retire for the night. Soho and Halfway have squeezed their tents near the rest of us. All of our tents are nearly touching. It's a tight fit.

"I hope I don't sleepwalk tonight. Overdrive, you know I sleep naked, right?" I joke as I crawl into my tent.

I stop and look out over the tents pitched so close together, like a village that will awaken tomorrow morning and move on to its next campsite and once again form another village. A Moving Village.

As I lie in my sleeping bag staring at the ceiling of my tent, my new nickname swims around in my head like a fish in a glass tank. *Mr. Fabulous . . .*

———

"What's a nero?" I ask as we start our 3.6-mile hike to Dicks Creek Gap, Georgia.

I know that a zero is a day off from hiking—zero miles for that day. But when Overdrive mentioned a nero to the closest trailhead, where Big Foot's dad awaits to drive us 11 miles to Hiawassee, the nearest town, I have to ask.

"It's a short hiking day," says my all-knowing hiking partner, Overdrive.

"Ah, a combination of near and zero," I say, feeling foolish that I didn't figure it out sooner.

So, a nero was what we did yesterday. We stopped to do laundry, but a shower was my true priority. I needed to sandblast the last few days of hiking off of me. Although I was cleaner than many other hikers—some of whom go a week or two without bathing—my daily birdbaths leave me far from my optimal cleanliness.

The night at the motel has left me feeling reenergized. Daddy Big Foot, which I have come to call Big Foot's dad, drives us back to the trailhead at Dicks Creek Gap. We strap on our packs and thank him for the lift. He's our first trail angel—someone, Overdrive has explained, who provides assistance or food to thru-hikers. We wave goodbye and start hiking in single file toward our first state line crossing.

Once again, Overdrive and I are moving faster than the rest of the Moving Village. I realize that I tend to mimic the pace of whoever is in front of me, whether it's a snail's pace, a steady pace, or Overdrive's rocket-like pace. We're currently moving full tilt, fueled by our excitement about reaching our first state border. But I'm not Overdrive, so eventually I slow down and steady my stride, letting the speedy hiker pull ahead. I'm definitely better at going up mountains than I was when I first started the AT, but Overdrive is—well, he's called Overdrive for a reason. He tears up the mountain as if it's a flat, rockless terrain. Mountains fear him, and children want to be him. One could hate or envy him for such power and speed. I choose to pretend that his legs are bionic.

Away he goes, leaving me alone with my thoughts, until I see a group of senior day hikers. I stand aside, giving them room to pass. They greet me and wish me luck on my journey. The last one in the group, a small woman who is slower than the rest, seemingly in her hundreds, is hiking with a cane and helped along by an aide. She stops, looks up at me, and asks me what my trail name is.

Believe it or not, it has taken some persuading for me to accept a trail name like *Mr. Fabulous*. I mean, what kind of egotistical person would . . . ?

"So, what's your trail name?" a day hiker asked me a few days ago.

"Um . . . well, *they* call me Mr. Fabulous," I replied sheepishly. "I didn't name myself, I promise," I quickly added.

To my relief, he smiled and offered some kind words. I got similar reactions from others. I'm finding that the name seems to evoke good humor, warmth, and affection. I must admit, I am amazed.

And now, this sweet elderly lady wants to know my trail name. "Mr. Fabulous, ma'am," I respond.

Our eyes meet, and her eyes widen with acknowledgment, as if she has been shown the answer to a mystery she has been pondering for decades. Then, without missing a beat, she says, "Oh, I've waited my entire life for a Mr. Fabulous."

She braces herself on her cane with one hand, and with the other she reaches up, touches my face, and guides me closer to her. Her hand is soft and smooth but cold on my cheek. The wrinkles on her face reveal a long life, but a youthful exuberance—an unmistakable childlike innocence—radiates through her eyes. Without another word, she kisses me on the cheek. Delighted with herself, she turns away and continues down the trail with a bounce in her step, leaving her aide chasing after her.

It occurs to me that my trail name is actually a fun introduction that clears the way for an engaging interaction with strangers. It's an optimistic name I can play with and make others feel *fabulous* with. I declare that from this moment on, I will proudly use my trail name—not only because I am *fabulous*, but because it seems to bring joy and amusement to those who hear it.

With newfound energy, I catch up to Overdrive and tell him about my enlightening encounter.

"I told you it's an awesome trail name!" he says with his uniquely *overdrive* response.

———————

A sign reading "NC/GA" greets us at our first border crossing. Overdrive and I are ecstatic. It's as if we just summited Katahdin. This is why I like hiking with this guy: He greets every milestone out here, even the little ones, with equal enthusiasm. We take pictures, posing in front of the old, weather-beaten sign, which has names carved into it.

"Our first state complete, Mr. Fabulous!"

"Our first state and only thirteen more to go. Wahoo!" I cheer as we high-five.

Soon, one by one, the other hikers in our group begin to show up and pose for their border picture. I'm not sure who started it, but we have taken up the habit of signaling our arrival with a *woot woot* call. When everyone is present, we take a group photo of the Moving Village: Overdrive, Big Foot, Downhill, Soho, Halfway, the Kid, Jolly 3-0, Doc, Trudger, Kevin (now Tower, named for his childlike love of fire towers and his tall frame), and a hiker who has finally accepted his trail name, Mr. Fabulous.

What's in a name?

Out here it defines you and tells your story, like the heroic Jolly 3-0 or the high-speed Overdrive or the tall-framed Big Foot. It also provides yet another reason to love the AT. Receiving a trail name is a way of accepting this experience and all that it will send your way.

CHAPTER 10

The Smokies

HOW DO I LOVE THEE? LET ME COUNT THE WAYS.

This is the sonnet I hear whenever Overdrive mentions the Great Smoky Mountains.

From day one he has raved about his previous Great Smoky Mountain hikes. A day doesn't go by without hearing Overdrive say, "I can't wait to get to the Smokies," or "We're so-and-so miles from the Smokies." If someone else mentions the Smoky Mountains, Overdrive's ebullience echoes throughout the camp.

At first I thought I was the only one to notice his obsession with his favorite mountain range, but when Doc, Three Week, and Tower mention Overdrive's long-winded stories of hiking the Smokies, we formulate a devious scheme.

"OK, so, every time he says *the Smokies* or anything to do with the Great Smoky Mountains, we should whistle," I suggest. "Let's see how long it takes him to figure it out."

The prank goes on for days and at times is so funny that it is difficult to whistle without laughing. Of course, Overdrive is so wrapped up in his praise of the Smokies that he hardly notices our meager attempts to conceal our laughter. After some time, just before we reach the Smokies, I reveal our silly antics.

"I had a feeling something was going on. I should have known you were up to some mischief, Mr. Fabulous," he says, taking it with his usual geniality.

Then, being the walking encyclopedia that he is, he adds, "Did you know that the Smokies are named that because of the mist and haze that encircle the mountains?"

"Hmm, I didn't know that. That's an interesting fact," and I begin to whistle "The Fishin' Hole" song.

Before I started this thru-hike, the only thing I knew about the Smokies was that it is a mountain range running along the Tennessee–North Carolina border. I pictured it as a land of wondrous beauty, which is what I imagined the whole Appalachian Trail would be like. But Overdrive's nonstop talk of the Smokies has me excited about this section of the AT, the 71 miles from Fontana Dam to Davenport Gap. It has to be something special if it left such a powerful impact on Overdrive. Because of that, for the first time, I believe this will be a day with no surprises, just a majestic hike waiting for me.

It's a sunny day, but I'm only aware of that fact when I cross a section of the trail not overshadowed by thick pine boughs. Rays of sunlight only penetrate the trail at openings in the dense forest. I look up when I reach a break in the canopy overhead and let the sun shine on my face. Towering trees lean over me like sentries guarding an entrance into the woods. Fallen trees covered in green moss litter the forest floor. The ones laid across the trail have been cut to make way for hikers. At one point, I hike under a dead tree. Its bare branches, several yards long, are shaped like the skeleton of a prehistoric beast. There's a poetic beauty in fallen trees. When these great perennial plants die, they nurture the ground they fall on and give life to other plants. Where else is the end of life so impactful, or so graceful in appearance?

Morning arrives with sounds of raindrops smacking the top of my tent. I'm buried in my sleeping bag. It's cold—I mean it is downright iceberg-making weather—and I stubbornly refuse to face it.

"Get up, Mr. Fabulous," I hear someone call.

It's known throughout the thru-hiking community that I lack early morning enthusiasm. The arctic conditions make this the rudest awakening yet.

"Leave me alone," I whimper.

I toss and turn, and after several tries, I finally force myself out of my sleeping bag. With my body trembling, I gather what I can into my backpack, then run to the shelter with it. Most of the Moving Village has left and started hiking. I sit on the picnic table with my arms wrapped around myself.

"You all right?" asks Soho, noticing a hopelessness I thought I was concealing.

"Yeah, no . . . I hate the Smokies," I whisper, not sure if I mean it but wanting to say it regardless.

"No, you don't," she replies.

"How do you know?"

She smiles and turns toward the trail. "I'll see you on the trail . . . Mr. Fabulous."

Overdrive plunks his backpack next to me.

"You're a Mr. Fabulous, you got this!" says my always-fired-up friend.

Does anything get this guy down? I wish something would.

"Yeah, well even Superman has a weakness. Hey, what's this I hear about there not being a privy out here?" I ask. I find it hard to believe that such a thing could be true.

"This is a hard-to-reach place . . . " Overdrive begins as he tightens the straps on his backpack.

"Is this going to be a long explanation?"

"Fine, you asked," he says with an adolescent expression of defiance. He continues preparing his pack.

"Ugh, OK . . . you just seem to have an answer for all my woes."

"Oh, Mr. Fabulous, it's not that bad."

"You're trying to convince someone who can't feel his fingertips and whose teeth won't stop chattering. So go ahead tell me: Why is this place privy-less?"

"Like I was saying, this is a hard area to reach, so the park eliminated privies because they require maintenance, and also because they don't receive as much use as those at shelters near more populated areas. The privy area, or cotton fields, are an experiment to see if those shelters can be sustained without a physical privy and with minimal impact on the environment."

"Wait . . . cotton fields?"

"You'll see," he answers with a smirk.

Damn, Overdrive, you lied about the Smokies.

I hold back tears of frustration. All I want is a warm morning and a privy. I would even make do with one or the other. But being faced with frosty rain and no decent place to take my morning crap—well, that's absolutely cruel.

Big Foot sees me shivering and in a mood. He suggests that I break down my tent in the covered extension of the shelter where I'm currently taking refuge. I take his advice, and after everyone leaves, I carry my tent out from the biting rain and into the shelter, where, with shaking hands, I begin to dismantle it.

By the time I finish my solitary breakfast, the rain stops, but the cold lingers. Reluctantly, I walk over to the designated non-privy area. I follow a path that leads me to an area with a thicket of thin, short trees. The ground is dotted with piles of exposed toilet paper, marking barely covered turds.

And there's your cotton field.

But instead of the softness of a real cotton field, it's a landmine of old turds. I give an inner whine. *Damn it, I don't wanna do this.* Still, I walk on, looking to the left and right of the pathway, trying to spot a section that has not been booby-trapped—or I should say, poopy-trapped. If I take one wrong step, it's all over.

Damn, it stinks.

I work my way to what looks like a promising area. Like a member of a bomb squad, I carefully maneuver around the doo-doo explosives until I find somewhat-unused dirt, with few visible signs of toilet paper. With a branch, I dig a hole deep enough to basket toilet paper and poop. As I lean against a tree, I recall my first privy use a few weeks back. That was a first for me, and I felt exposed then, but this is something else entirely.

When I finish, I walk back to the shelter where my backpack awaits me. I grip my hiking poles with numb fingers and wet gloves. It's 10 A.M., and everyone else left hours ago. If there's anything that can slow me down even more in the morning, it's this harsh, damp weather. Yet there's nothing I can do about it but move forward.

It's our last day in the Smokies, and I couldn't be more thrilled. I'm finally leaving this temperamental section of the AT, and I determine that today will be a great day. Although the terrain here in the Smokies has been fairly easy, and the views have indeed been awe-inspiring, the unrelenting cold nights and even colder mornings have been too much for me. If the entire Appalachian Trail was like this, my shivering ass would be headed back to the big city before you could say *frostbite*. I'm not made for this type of weather. My forebears are from the tropics, and an affinity for warm climates is in my blood.

Even so, last night Overdrive announced that the weather we've been having is mild compared to past seasons.

"What?" I said. "You left that little detail out when you were praising the do-no-wrong Smokies. I'm beginning to think I was bamboozled."

"Ha, you're funny, Mr. Fabulous," Overdrive said as he walked away.

"Punk," I whispered to myself.

I'm not up against the clock, and although I'm eager to be far away from this frosty land, I decide to try to enjoy my final day on this mountain range. So, when I finally poke my head out of my tent, I'm not surprised that my hiking comrades are all gone. An hour later, with hip-hop music playing in my earbuds, I'm groovier than groovy, feelin' the rhythm and jammin' to the tunes.

Looks like it's going to be a sweet hike.

And the day is a beauty—until the dusty trail turns downhill in a switch-back. Feeling overly buoyant, I mindlessly attempt to step over a log meant to provide easier footing. But in my haste, my left trekking pole slides over the log step, and I lose my balance.

This is not happening! This never happens to m—

In a quick, continuous motion, my backpack, now top-heavy, propels me forward, causing me to lose control of my footing. I'm thrust down, and the descent magnifies my fall. I fly through the air long enough to attempt a twist of my body in an effort to land on my pack instead of my face. I brace for impact. *This is going to hurt.* I hit the ground with a bounce, my arms and legs flinging wildly like a rag doll's. I'm surrounded by a puff of dust that's a miniature minefield explosion. I wait long enough for the dust to settle, then I see that my left leg is above me, draped over a thick tree root. My other leg is resting out of my sight. I lie there, waiting for the pain to reach my brain so I can assess what part of my body is damaged. When pain doesn't come . . . *Wait, am I paralyzed?* That fear dissipates once I start to move my arms and pat myself.

How did that happen?

I'm not sure, and actually, I don't care. I'm just glad I have full control of my limbs after such a murderous fall.

Unbelievable. Smokies, you couldn't even let me enjoy this final day. You're such a vengeful mountain range.

I laugh while still lying on the ground, strapped to my pack. I must look like an upside-down tortoise.

Amazingly, I don't hurt anywhere. I slowly loosen the backpack from my shoulders, then reach over to a side pocket and pull out an energy bar. I unwrap it and take a bite while watching the last of the dust particles dissipate far above me. I slide out of the backpack straps and rock to the left, then to the right, pushing myself off the ground. I check for broken bones, take a look back at my dusty pack, and give a loud roar of laughter. I leave my turtle shell where it lies and walk over to a clearing with a view that promises to take my mind off of my abrupt plummet.

How can you be so beautiful, yet so cruel? I wonder as I gaze into the face of the Smokies.

I see row upon row of mountains. Although it's mid-April, the closer mountains are covered in various autumn colors. In the valleys, light green trees flow for miles, like a river swerving through and around the mountains. This visual bliss clears a part of my mind that has been muddled by my weather discomforts. I get it now . . . and all the cold mornings and bodily bruises can never take it away from me.

I finish my energy bar and grab my dusty pack, thanking it for cushioning my fall. I need to salvage some goodness from this hike, or my experience in the Smokies will forever be followed by a poop emoji. So it's an optimistic attitude for the rest of my day.

Peace, love, and all th—curses!

My left ankle rolls outward. I manage to catch it before it causes any damage.

"Damn it! Now I'm not crazy! You're not going to let me leave in peace, are you?" I shout. I'd be at a loss for words if a hiker happened to walk up and see me flailing my arms and yelling at the mountains.

I hurriedly remove my pack, toss it to the side, and squeeze my eyes shut. Then I take a deep breath. I slowly open my eyes, and once again, I'm taken aback by the splendor of what I see. Mountains, older and grander than I am, reach inside me and set free the strain I feel. The mountains that have given me such heartache also fill my heart with joy.

Love—such a fickle thing. I strap on my pack and try again.

———

Freshly out of the Smokies, I hit a dirt road, where a couple of hikers are offering trail magic: the free goodies and sometimes favors bestowed by trail angels.

A blanket is laid out with brownies, oatmeal cream sandwich cookies, and various Tastykakes, all spilling out of a shopping bag. Also on offer are cheese calzones, wrapped in aluminum foil and cooked in a campfire, which pleases this New Yorker. I've had plenty of those in pizzerias in Brooklyn. And they're using a portable grill to make zuzu, a mini Snickers bar fried in a cinnamon roll and topped with frosting.

My heart warns me, *If you love me, you will not ingest that artery clogger!* But my stomach pleads with hunger pangs that only stop when I wolf down the zuzu.

Sorry, heart. I'm a weak man.

After an hour, I pull myself away. With 7 more miles of hiking ahead of me and a belly full of trail magic, I begin my trek up Snowbird Mountain. The elevation at the summit is 4,263 feet, which seems extreme, especially in my condition, but that doesn't register in my euphoric state. My only objective is to trek up and over this mountain to Groundhog Creek Shelter, where my group will probably be asleep before I arrive.

Darkness creeps in, taking hold of what is left of the daylight.

"*Woot woot,*" I call as I approach camp a little after 7 P.M.

A half hour longer and I would have had to pull out my headlamp. The thick forest is blocking all light from the setting sun.

"*Woot woot,*" I hear in response.

Standing around a campfire is most of the Moving Village. It was a long 17.6 miles of emotions crammed into one day, a day that felt like multiple days, a day without Overdrive, Soho, Downhill, and the rest of the gang. I slip off my pack and launch into the tale of my rocky affair with the Smokies. I tell the story using hand gestures and a physical reenactment. Am I sensationalizing events? Perhaps, but I'm only reflecting the effect this day had on me. Campfires and storytelling are two of the things we treasure most out here. Watching the smiles on the faces of my fellow hikers, I finish the tale of the wicked beauty of the Great Smoky Mountains and our brawling love.

CHAPTER 11

Becoming an Unlikely Thru-hiker

It's true that before I started hiking the AT, I knew next to nothing about backpacking. Even after several weeks of hiking, I'm still flabbergasted by the simplest of trail lessons. I'm gradually noticing, however, that my lack of experience isn't the only reason I'm attracting attention on the trail. Back home in New York, I'd thought surely there are other persons of color who have the wild notion of living in the woods for months. Turns out I was wrong. Like watching *The Andy Griffith Show* and not realizing how few blacks are onscreen, it didn't occur to me that hiking in general is a predominantly white pastime. I've come to discover we're a rare sight out here. Diversity has not yet reached the AT, although the trail does seem ready, wide-eyed, and with open arms.

I've also started wondering what fellow hikers think of me upon first meeting. I usually don't wonder for long: Most people come right out with it. While we're in the wicked Smokies, on our way up to Clingmans Dome, an older-looking southbound hiker approaches Overdrive and me. He stops in front of us with purpose. "You know, I've been hiking the trails of the Smokies for over fourteen years, and you are," he says, turning to me, "only the seventh black thru-hiker I have ever seen."

The unexpected honesty takes me aback, but it's clear his candor doesn't stem from prejudice. His expression is friendly and kind. His is a look that belongs to a man who goes fishing with his buddy Andy, the local small-town sheriff.

Even so, and even though his words are far from malicious, I'd prefer it if the greeting could go unsaid. He is pleased with his observation—so much so it doesn't occur to him that skin color is not a factor for me in this venture, or for anything else in my life.

Yeah, I have dreadlocks, café con leche skin, and Afro–Puerto-Rican-ness running through my veins. It doesn't mean diddly-squat. I'm no different from my friend Overdrive, standing right next to me, hiking the same trail with the same goal.

I'm not offended. How could I be offended at the benevolence emitted from the senior hiker? Instead, I choose to take his reaction as one of jubilation, a celebration at seeing a fellow human being from a different part of the world hiking the AT, even if that different part of the world is New York City and not another continent or planet.

The joy he gets from seeing me out here in turn becomes my joy, and I begin to realize how important it is for me to be on this trail.

———————

I catch her gaze as I cross the parking lot of a small-town supermarket. With her head slightly tilted to the right, as if it's giving her a better understanding of what she is seeing, she moves closer to me. She's pop-eyed—not because she's frightened, although she sure is scaring the hell out of *me*. It's like a shot in an old black-and-white thriller, when the camera catches a close-up of the ghoul slowly approaching its victim.

Damn, she's creeping me out. Does she know me? What's her deal?

She stops a few feet in front of me, and before I can make a run for it, she says, "Hi."

"Hi," I tentatively reply.

I feel my lips quiver. I hope she didn't notice.

"Are you thru-hiking?" she asks.

"Uh, yeah."

She's beautiful, with short black hair and skin a shade lighter than mine. She continues to stare as if studying my face. I get a sense that she wants to tell me something but can't decide if she can trust me with it. I'm just as lost for words.

"I'm Steps."

"I'm Mr. . . . ." I swallow, my mouth feeling dry all of a sudden.

What's my name?

I draw a blank, her beauty and her poltergeist stares making me nervous.

"I'm Mr. Fabulous," I blurt, as if attempting to be the first to answer a question.

She nods as if in agreement, but she doesn't seem to hear me. An inner conversation has her full attention.

"OK . . . nice . . . meeting you," I say, unsure how to converse in this eccentric way.

"Bye," she says, still wide-eyed. She flashes a big smile that would, in a different setting, be flattering. At this moment, however, it recalls the smile the Joker gives his victims before he shoots them in the face with his long-barreled gun.

I take a couple of steps backward, turn around, and then realize that I'm going the wrong way.

I turn back around. "Oh, yeah, this way," I whisper and scurry away.

I go over in my head what just happened. Unsaid words seem to linger in the air, like an indistinguishable scent.

A few days later, when I get a chance to have a real conversation with Steps, I learn that she is not as nutty as our first encounter suggested. In fact, she is smart and free-spirited. She hikes the trail without rules, in her own way and not on a set schedule. Later, the story I hear is that she embraced a black female day hiker and thanked her for being on the trail. And just like that, it all makes sense: She was astonished—and in her way, excited—to see someone of color thru-hiking. I still can't get used to the fact that black thru-hikers are so rare out here. I think of my life and of the people closest to me back home. Most, if not all, of my family and friends have never camped or hiked up a mountain to see a breathtaking view at the summit. Growing up, the Appalachian Trail was as distant as the Milky Way.

The realization that I may be somewhat of an anomaly on the Appalachian Trail gives me much to ponder. Moreover, it sparks in me a strong desire to share my experience with those who have never heard of this long-distance trek. If more individuals like me, the backcountry-challenged and the urbanites, were aware of this astonishing trail, then perhaps there would be more outdoorsy types of all colors—and fewer unlikely thru-hikers.

CHAPTER 12

Not a Rasta!

OVERDRIVE, THE KID, AND I HIKE 13 MILES IN LESS THAN FOUR HOURS to a tiny town called Hot Springs, in North Carolina. It's the size of three Manhattan blocks. Blink and you'll miss the first town the Appalachian Trail goes straight through.

Our knees are sore and our legs are aching, but our stomachs are prodding us forward. We power through for one reason and one reason only: to quiet our raging hunger. By noon we're eating two servings of everything and anything that Spring Creek Tavern has to offer.

On our way back to Laughing Heart Lodge, the hostel where we're staying for the night, I see a scruffy, familiar face crossing the main street a few yards ahead. He smirks, recognizing me before I realize that it's Swiss.

"Whaaat!" I exclaim.

I knew him for only one day, the first day of my adventure, but now I feel as if I'm reunited with a long-lost family member.

"You're alive," Swiss says.

"You sound surprised. Was your plan to leave me for dead? Where's Josh and Mike? Is Josh's trail name Jaybird and Mike's Polaris? Are you staying in town? Did you miss me? Wanna dance?" I realize that I'm hitting him with loads of questions and not stopping for answers.

I've been following his register entries for weeks. I would see Swiss's name with two other trail names and have deduced those are my other two Springer Mountain pals.

"OK, let's start with no dancing," replies Swiss. "Next: Josh was carrying a bird encyclopedia, so yeah, he's Jaybird. Polaris, though, isn't Mike. He's a hiker we met a few days after we left Springer. I haven't seen Mike since a bear ripped open our food bags . . . "

"What?" Overdrive says.

Swiss explains that after they separated from me, they camped at Wolf Laurel, just after Neels Gap. That night, a bear was able to reach the food bags they had hung in a tree and rip through them. They had just resupplied, so the bear made off with everything but peanut butter and coffee.

"That's all I need!" I jest.

"We gathered what was left," Swiss continues, "and split it among ourselves. A few hikers gave us what they could. That was the last time we saw Mike."

"Dang, that's rough," I say. "Hey, Swiss, we're headed back to the hostel to wash the trail off us. See you at the tavern tonight?"

"I'll be there."

We shake hands and pull each other in for a quick embrace.

Overdrive, the Kid, and I get to the hostel as the rest of the Moving Village begins to arrive.

It's 2 o'clock, and with my hiker appetite sated for the time being, I get ready for a needed shower. Yesterday when I boasted about the shower I was going to take when I got to town, a female hiker I have never seen before said, "I just took a shower three days ago. There's no need for another one so soon." If I had heard a female say such a thing a month ago in New York City, I would have thought she was nasty. But being the thru-hikers that we are, I casually said, "Oh, that's cool you're still fresh."

Yet for me, a day without a wash is a day too many. I refuse to miss a shower—or at least a rinse of the pits and private parts. A handful of water gets me by until I'm able to take a full shower. I could never get used to a day without washing, even if I wanted to. The discomfort of sweat and dirt sticking to my body would keep me up all night.

I stay in the shower longer than usual, enjoying our first zero after almost a month on the trail. A day of rest will be good for my mind, feet, and soul.

———

The tavern is alive with music and filled with hikers and locals. Overdrive orders us beers as I check out the scene. I see hiker faces I have yet to meet.

"Rastaman! What's up?" I hear someone say behind me.

A thick, round-faced guy with a nose that looks like it has been broken several times accosts me. Although he looks mean, like a bulldog, his eyes say otherwise.

Two taller guys join him, all sporting some form of dreadlocked hairstyle. The short, boxer-faced guy has big, thick, untamed locks, giving him a madman look. One of the others has hair that's longer but just as messy. The third, a younger pretty-boy type, has a few loose locks, as if he's trying out the hairstyle for the weekend. They seem gleefully drunk.

"Hey," I respond. I'm the only dark-skinned guy with dreadlocks at a bar in a small Southern town, so yeah, I assume he's talking to me.

"It's actually Mr. Fabulous, if we're using nicknames," I add with a smile.

Ignoring my response, Bull Dog leans over and says, a bit too closely into my right ear, "You got ganja?"

The question is meant to be discreet, but he is too drunk to realize that he is yelling. The bar, however, is filled with the sound of live music and energetic conversations, so there's no fear of anyone hearing us.

I have been asked about ganja several times since I've been on the trail. I've grown tired of explaining: No, I'm not a Rasta, and I don't smoke or have ganja. The topic is getting old, and by the look of their inebriated state, these guys wouldn't get it anyway.

"Nah, I left it in my tent," I respond.

Hey, if I can't get away from the hogwash, then I'm going to roll with it.

"Oh," he says, with one eye squinting and the other raised a bit as he sways back and forth. An image of Popeye the Sailor runs through my mind.

With perfect timing, Overdrive arrives with our beers. I excuse myself and we go in search of a place to sit. I look back and see that Popeye the Bull Dog remains staring at the spot where I was standing until one of his buddies nudges him and hands him a beer.

Overdrive and I settle at a table with three section hikers that I met this morning. We chat for a bit before two of them walk over to the bar to order more drinks. Within seconds, the two unoccupied seats are taken, and another chair is pulled up to the table. It seems as if the three messy dreadlock guys were watching, waiting to swoop right in.

"You look like our close friend Rob," says Bull Dog.

He has had way too much to drink, not only tonight, but it seems most of his life. His leathery face sits on his youth like proof that he's abused some narcotics too.

"Oh, I look like your friend?" I ask, not knowing how to respond.

"Yeah, we miss him. He's not here with us," he says to my shirt.

He's not making eye contact.

"Oh, what happened?" I say, expecting a tragic story.

"He left us . . . lives in Florida . . . got a job."

"Oh, well aren't you happy for him?" I ask.

"*He's* not happy. We're trying to get him back," Bull Dog says. *Back to what? Doing nothing but smoking ganja? Sounds like your friend got his life together.*

It's sad, kind of. These guys are actually harmless, friendly fellas, like delinquent hippies.

"Mr. Fabulous, can I buy you a beer?" asks Stringer, the youngest and the only one of the three addressing me by my trail name.

He seems to be enjoying himself tonight but not making this a lifestyle. Still, he's quite smashed.

Hours pass, the band ends their set, and the musicians begin to pack their instruments. It's 1 A.M. and the bar is closing, but customers continue drinking and making their pleas for one last round.

"Mr. Fabulous," says Stringer.

Out of the three, he is the coolest and most courteous. Earlier, when he returned with a beer for me, we talked for a while, and although he sometimes lost track of his thoughts, it was better conversation than what his dread friends were offering up.

"Stringer, what's up, dude?"

He's looking more trashed than ever as he flashes a sharp smile at me.

"Mr. Fabulous, did you have fun tonight?" he asks.

"I did. What about you?"

"Look at me," he says, swaying left to right, and then opening his arms as if to show how grand he is. He spills some of the beer he is holding. He looks around to see if anyone saw his beer-spilling folly. He hugs his beer, to protect it from another spill.

"Hey, Rasta!"

Yes, Bull Dog? my annoyed inner voice responds.

"Where you . . . stay tonight?" he slurs.

"At Laughing Heart," I say, ignoring the alias he has given me.

"We're ... makin' ganja pancakes ... morrow mornin'. You come join us. We're campin' by river," he utters with closed eyes.

I'm barely able to decipher his mangled words.

"Ganja pancakes ... woo, who can resist that?" He doesn't notice my sarcasm.

Funny thing: Up to that point, I wasn't even sure they were actually doing any kind of hiking. I'm still not convinced that they are.

Meanwhile, my conversations with other hikers and locals continue. In fact, it takes a lot to tear myself away from it all. When I finally step out into the night, it's nearly 2 A.M.

I'm headed back to the hostel when I see someone moving a few yards away, wobbling more than walking. The drunken figure stops to stare at the closest house, as if deciding whether to walk up to the porch and knock on the door. He stumbles on, stops, then looks across the street. He turns his head in my direction and notices my approach. Turning too quickly, he loses his equilibrium, struggles to stand, and falls backward onto the grassy lawn. He sits staring over at me.

"Mr. Fabulous . . . ."

"Stringer, what's going on?"

My young hiker friend looks as lost as a child in a crowded mall.

"I'm ... trying to find ... " he begins, searching for words he can't seem to find, either.

His eyes fight for focus. He's aware of my presence, but I don't think he actually sees me.

"Stringer, where are you staying tonight?" I ask.

He gradually shakes his head in an attempt to clear his thoughts. He tries to stand but falls back down with the weight of his pack. He tries again. I reach down and place my arm under his, guiding him up and steadying his stance. I free his tangled arms from the straps of his backpack and swing it over my right shoulder.

"Let me carry this for you."

He puts his arm over my shoulder to steady himself, and I wrap my arm around him and guide him along.

"You're coming with me," I say, not waiting for an answer.

He obviously is not capable of getting home by himself, and I'm not about to leave him out here alone. I'm tempted to ask him where his so-called friends are, but now is obviously not the time, and it's not my place to lecture him about the company he keeps.

"Mr. Fabulous, thanks. I had way too . . . ." He loses his train of thought, then finds it again: " . . . much to drink. I didn't mean to . . . I'm . . . thanks, Mr. Fabulous."

He's in his early twenties, but right now he's just a child to me. I want to get him someplace where he can sleep off this mess he's in.

"It's cool. You can pitch your tent in the hostel's yard," I explain.

At the hostel I direct him to the grassy lawn where I'm sure he's going to cowboy camp under a tree, clearly too wasted to pitch a tent.

"Are you good, kid?" I ask before I head into the hostel for a shower.

"Yeah . . . thanks."

"Well, good night, then," I say walking away.

"Goodnight . . . thank you," he says, swaying back. He leans forward like Michael Jackson in the "Smooth Criminal" video and then stands and straightens out. I'm impressed that he is still standing.

I continue walking until I hear him say, "Thank you. I have intimate love for you, Mr. Fabulous!"

I turn around to see him waving at me. He drops to the ground under the tree and begins to pull his sleeping bag out of his pack.

Intimate love?

Must be some hip lingo I'm unaware of. Could be his version of *one love*? Regardless, coming from him, it sounds genuine.

"And I you, my friend," I softly say.

Intimate love? I can get down with that.

CHAPTER 13

And Then the Snow Came

AFTER MY NERO INTO ERWIN, TENNESSEE, YESTERDAY, I'M IN NO HURRY to leave the comforts of the hostel today. A forecasted snowstorm has given me the excuse I need to delay. At 2:30 P.M., my latest start ever, I finally shake off my lax disposition and hike out of town. My trail group left five hours ago. There's no catching up to them today, and I'm OK with that. It's why, after 10 miles, I settle on a campsite near the trail.

This will be my first night camping solo in the woods. Until this moment, when I am actually left alone in a dark forest that swallows everything around it, I hadn't really considered how I would feel. The wilderness sounds that I've grown accustomed to now seem menacing. The security of being with other humans gone, my mind conjures up creatures that seek to do me harm. I'm not far from the road, so there's also the possibility of a serial killer discovering my solitary camp.

In the evening, pitch blackness surrounds me. Everything seems darker than usual. I constantly pause while I eat my dinner, trying to work out if the sound I just heard was the wind rustling branches, or if someone or something is creeping toward my tent.

How am I going to get through this night? is my last thought before I drift into an exhausted sleep.

When morning finally arrives, I feel rejuvenated. I survived my first night alone.

Ha—that wasn't hard at all.

With the night peril behind me, I am filled with a half-baked bravado.

I pack my gear and head out for another solo hike. There's not a single hiker on the trail, and the song "All by Myself" plays on a loop in my head. Although I prefer the company of fellow hikers, there's something about hiking alone that rejuvenates me. When alone, there's no one to observe whether I'm fast or slow or tired or hungry. I can be any hiker I please. One moment I'm a hiking machine, storming up and down mountains with ease; the next I'm a student of nature, studying the clouds as they drift slowly across the sky.

After a day without seeing a single soul, I spend another night alone. This time it's a bit easier to endure. I'm up at 6 A.M., the earliest I've ever stirred out of my sleeping bag. But it's cold and dark, and I immediately want to fall back to sleep.

My plan for the day is to reach Overmountain Shelter, a large red barn that was used as the filming location for the horror movie *The People Under the Stairs* and has been converted into a hiker shelter. Being the movie buff that I am, I'm eager to see the set. I also want to pass the Moving Village while they sleep, get to Overmountain Shelter, and surprise them with my presence when they arrive. But at this egregiously early hour, I'm finding it hard to imagine why I wanted to do such a thing. I'm groggy, unfocused, and too cold to care. Still, I'm hit with a nagging sense that I should get to the red shelter early, before the forecasted snow begins to fall.

After a couple of attempts, I force myself out of my tent. I gather my gear and head out. Within minutes, I pass the quiet shelter that is housing my slumbering trail family. It begins to drizzle, but that doesn't bother me; what does is the chill that begins to creep through my glove liner. There suddenly doesn't seem to be any way to keep my hands warm. The hike up Roan Highlands—the last stretch of the AT that is over 6,000 feet in elevation until Mount Washington in New Hampshire—with no switchbacks adds to my discomfort.

I make a right on the blue-blazed trail that will take me 0.3 mile to the shelter. I'm low on water, but the fog and the snow, which begins to blow in with a steady wind, hide the water source. Still, it doesn't matter; I'm way too cold to attempt filtering water with my pump. I'll have to make do with the little water I have.

As I reach the area where the red shelter should be, I see nothing but a thick fog a few feet ahead of me. But gradually, as I move forward, I see a red structure breaking through the fog.

With the damp, cold weather and a disquieting darkness, the secluded barn feels spooky. I slowly walk through it and up the wooden steps to the second floor. I recall scenes that I imagine were shot in certain areas of the barn and begin to feel like I'm in an actual horror movie. A chill runs through me, and I wish someone were here to hold me or to tell me I'm being silly.

I walk around the barn in search of a tentsite, but the thought of pitching my tent in this cold seems impossible. Stiff, frozen fingers will be of little use to me in the morning when I'm trying to break camp. I play with the thought of pitching my tent on the second floor of the barn. The space looks large enough to fit a dozen tents. I'm sure I won't be taking an unnecessary amount of space from other hikers who plan to spend the night here.

Daammn . . . it's so cold that my dreadlocks are freezing into icicles. An unwanted image arises of a dreadlock breaking right off of my head.

That would suck.

Flurries continue to fall, and the wind blows into the barn with a bite. *That settles it.* I go with the impulse to pitch my tent inside the barn.

———————

"Anyone up there?" I hear Downhill call up from the bottom of the barn steps.

I've been here for an hour, and he's the first hiker to join me. I poke my head over the railing and shout down, "Hey, keep it down. I'm trying to sleep up here. Oh, and close the door behind you! What, were you raised in a barn?"

I've been waiting to say that since I got here.

"Mr. Fabulous!" he says, carefully climbing up the steep steps. "How did you get here before us?" He reaches the top step and looks around.

"They don't call me Mr. Fabulous for nothing. Good to see ya, old man." I walk up to my trail dad and give him a big, stinky, cold, hiker hug.

He looks over at my tent. "Good idea, pitching your tent up here."

"Yeah, it's freezing out there. Where's Overdrive?" I ask.

"He's at the water source."

Downhill doesn't waste any time finding a spot to pitch his tent. Overdrive soon arrives and the rest of the Moving Village begins to trickle in. Before long, the barn is filled with tents, and I'm feeling good about being back with a bunch of hikers. The only one missing is Soho. No one has seen her today. She must have moved farther ahead, perhaps into town.

The wind picks up outside. It then starts blowing into a large open window on the second floor, where nearly a dozen tents now reside. Big Foot offers the Kid's tarp to block the wind and promises to buy him a new one when we get into town. Overdrive covers some of the opening with the tarp, and it does stop the wind but not the cold. Without a doubt, it's the coldest night of my AT journey—something I didn't think possible after the Smokies.

———————

In the morning, the temperature makes last night's cold feel like a pleasant breeze on a tropical island. I'm dumbfounded by that realization.

I hear hikers unzipping their tents and someone says, "Whoa, there's snow all over our stuff."

Not what I want to hear.

When I finally step out of my tent, I'm shocked by what I see. The tarp was not enough to stop the snow from blowing in through wide gaps in the wall. My tent is covered in snow and frost. Both pairs of my hiking socks, which I left out to dry with the rest of my clothes, are frozen hard as stone, my shirt and pants stiff as cardboard. The little water I had left in my Platypus is now a block of ice. For the first time on this wondrous Appalachian Trail thru-hike, I don't want to be here.

I stand still in a daze, uncertain where to start. I search the moving bodies as they quickly get ready to step outside, where the snow is still falling. I can't seem to grasp a clear thought.

What is going on here? It's April 23 and there's a snowstorm?

A breeze stings my fingertips, snapping me out of my dazed state. I grab my iceberg-covered clothes and climb back into my tent. After a quick shiver, I take a deep breath before I close my eyes and scrabble into my freezing shirt and pants.

Keeping my eyes closed, I picture a warm sandy beach in Puerto Rico, but a gust of wind blows against my tent, turning the image of sand into snow. I open my eyes and step back out of my tent. My socks are too iced over to wear. Overdrive offers a pair of his dirty but dry socks when he sees what has happened to mine. I kindly refuse his offer.

I'm not that desperate. Not yet, anyway.

Instead, I decide to wear the thin pair of socks that I sleep in. Then I try to put on my rock-hard boots, but it's impossible to squeeze my feet into them. I bang my boots on the floor in an attempt to soften them up. I try again, but they don't give. Everyone else has gotten his or her boots on, so I know it's feasible. I'm able to get my toes in the stonelike boot, but that's all. The cold and frustration blur my vision, and I wonder if my tears will turn to ice and freeze my eyelids shut.

Nearly defeated, I give one more push, finally getting my foot into the boot, almost breaking a pinky toe in the process. I spend several more minutes on the other boot. My frozen boots feel like ice sculptures, only not as lovely as the ones at weddings or fancy parties.

"It's only a few miles—real easy, no mountains, Fabulous."

I turn to Halfway. She sees my struggle and attempts to ease my mind.

"Easy. You can make it," she adds.

I adore that girl.

"It's not that, it's the cold I'm having trouble with."

"It's OK," she says, nodding her head as if showing me how to agree with her.

I give her a reassuring smile and nod. I turn and begin the process of breaking down my tent in the numbing cold.

"How are we supposed to hike in this?" I say to no one in particular.

"One step at a time," says Big Foot in a come-on-and-stop-being-a-wuss tone.

Coming from Big Foot, it's the kick in the ass I need to get me going. With my giant friend, there's no holding back—just a good dose of reality.

Also, what's the big deal? No one's going to freeze to death out here . . . right?

The Moving Village has decided to hike in pairs, and they have all left. The Kid and Overdrive offer to wait for me, but my gear is still lying all over the barn, so I tell them to go on ahead, and I'll catch up.

"Leave footprints in the snow for me to follow," I yell after them. "Or bread crumbs," I whisper to myself.

The truth is, if I don't get those boots on, I'll have been tempted to do a zero at the barn. But that would be a lame move. I won't cave because the weather isn't perfect. Didn't I realize this might happen at some point?

Man up, Fabulous . . . you have a trail name to live up to.

I finally get myself together and start down the steps, when suddenly . . .

Damn, not now. And not here.

There's no question about it: I have to poop. But the privy at this shelter has no door, and worse yet, it doesn't even have a roof. It's just a toilet seat over a hole, surrounded by three 5-by-5-foot corrugated metal sheets for walls.

Man, I gotta go!

As if this morning wasn't bad enough, I now have to bare my ass out here in the blistering cold.

While I squat inches over the porcelain toilet seat, I wonder why they bothered to make this look like a real toilet. Is it an illusion-of-comfort thing for those who can only poo in a bathroom and not outside over a hole in the ground?

My butt cheeks are freezing, and the snow blows hard into my face. I can't help but laugh at my situation. I'm almost tempted to take a selfie, but then I think twice about it. Who would I share it with?

———

Fifteen minutes into my hike, my toes begin to warm up. Overdrive's declaration, "Warmth cometh with hiking," does not sound as ridiculous as it once did. Still, I'm wearing four layers of clothing—every single piece I've been carrying with me.

The snow looks beautifully serene on the ground and on the branches of trees. I stop to take a photo. It's not bad hiking in the snow; in fact, I find that I like it. It's sort of . . . magical.

I reach an opening in the forest and step out onto a bald, treeless summit called Little Hump Mountain. On a clear and sunny day, this spot must offer a stunning view, but at this moment the wind is fiercely blowing snow. The magic has turned into wicked wizardry. Every few steps, I have to stop and brace myself or risk being blown away. I look to my left, then to my right, and see only emptiness. There's nothing but a sheet of whiteness, like what you see when you peer out the window of an airplane that's flying through thick clouds. The sight is both enchanting and terrifying.

The wind presses hard on my pack, threatening to push me right into the white abyss. If it succeeds in knocking me off the path into the thick ice fog, I'm done for. I won't find my way back onto the Appalachian Trail. The thought of being swept into nothingness grows stronger, as does the wind on my back. I fight for every step, trying not to lose my balance.

Looking down, I notice that the footprints I was following are starting to fade. The brutal wind is blowing fresh snow onto the trail, covering the tracks. The icy snow cuts me like fragments of broken glass. The strap on my rain jacket hood whips my left cheek with a sting, and just when I think the wind can't get any more vicious, it does exactly that. I stop, lift my head, and yell.

"Is that all you have? Blow, damn it, blow! I'm not afraid of you!"

A flash of fury runs through me, but I instantly regret my words, like a child who snaps at a parent and then quickly realizes it was a dim-witted retort.

The wind responds to my childish rant with a strength that nearly rips my right pole out of my grasp. I'm scared, but I hoot and yell some more in crazed defiance. This action draws out a grit from within me. Whether real or imagined, it's something I cling to. A renewed energy flows through me with every howl and hoot.

This is the toughest and meanest hike yet. In the midst of this madness, I think of my friends back home in their warm New York apartments. I yearn to be there now, ensconced in the comfort of my daily routine.

Lost in my reverie, I suddenly find myself in the precise predicament I've been struggling to avoid.

Shiii—this can't be! I lost the trail. I friggin' lost the trail!

I stand looking down at my snow-covered boots. I slowly and deliriously do a 360-degree turn, failing to find the trail. The ground is nothing but a sheet of solid snow. The winter fog touches the distant ground, giving it an endless appearance. I can't tell where the ground and fog actually meet. Hysteria flows through my body and mind as I find myself in the middle of oblivion.

How can this be? Damn it, why am I out here alone? Why didn't I leave with the others? Why, why, why . . . ? Stop, Derick, stop!

I struggle to regain my composure. I swallow built-up emotions that want to come out in a blind panic. It takes all the strength I can muster to steady myself and focus my brain on a solution. My mind is twisted with thoughts of hopelessness and despair, and part of me wants to give up. My entire body is shaking; it's my only movement because I don't dare take another step. I wait for what seems like an eternity for some form of clarity to take over. Somewhat calm, I take one large step to my left—and poof, I'm back on the trail.

"The trail, the trail, the trail, oh god, the trail!" I say to myself, my eyes welling up.

I don't know why I took that side step to my left. My body reacted before I knew what was happening. If there was ever a time when I felt a spiritual guardian watching over me, this is it. I'm not out of this mess, but at least I'm not making it worse by wandering farther off the trail.

I can make out a hiker ahead of me. He looks to be tall, with long legs that are nonetheless moving him deceptively slowly. I'm not moving with any swiftness myself, but I manage to catch up to the hiker.

"Your rain cover is flying off," I shout to him.

"What?" I think he responds, but the wind muffles our voices, making it difficult to hear.

"Your pack cover," I yell and point.

He doesn't get it, so I grab his rain cover and secure it back on his pack.

He nods a thank you and signals for me to walk ahead. It's not a good time for idle chat, so we push on. The footprints I was following are now completely gone, and the trail is beginning to follow suit. I can barely discern the difference between the AT and the open field.

As I reach the top of a hill, the trail now plays another nasty trick: There's a fork in the trail without a white blaze in sight. I stand staring at both trails, hoping a snow apparition will present itself and show the correct way. But before that happens, the hiker I passed earlier catches up.

No need for him to ask. "I have no idea," I yell.

He studies both trails as I did and comes up empty.

This is a crazy predicament. We are fools to be out here hiking in this treacherous weather.

Wanting to continue moving and not stay still in this intense storm, I suggest that he take the right trail, I take the left, and the first one to see a white blaze will run back and tell the other.

We part, and I struggle to find a white blaze in this space of white. But after a few steps, I can barely make out a 5-foot wooden pole with a faded white blaze, which is how the trail is marked on mountain balds and in fields without trees.

I run back, yelling for the hiker to take the trail I am on. I'm not sure if he hears me, but he happens to look back and sees me waving. We make it down into the trees, and just like that, the storm dies down and we're back in a winter wonderland.

"I heard someone yelling earlier. Was that you?" my fellow storm survivor asks.

"Oh, yeah," I say, feeling ridiculous. "I know it may sound weird, but the yelling kind of helped me get through the storm."

"Hey, whatever works," he says, now leading the way.

He finishes his day at a nearby hostel, and I safely reach the trailhead, where Daddy Big Foot and his truck are waiting, a welcome sight indeed. I climb in the back and notice Soho is still missing.

"Any word on Soho?" I ask Halfway.

"No, nothing," she says, looking troubled.

Later in the evening, Halfway gets a call from Soho. She's safe, but she spent the night at a rugged campsite on the descent of Hump Mountain, right in the heart of the snowstorm. So, after waking up surrounded by an endless expanse of snow and no idea where the trail was, she had to be rescued by the park authorities and taken to the nearest hostel.

"What?" I say astounded.

"I'm not the most experienced hiker, but what I do know is that it is the hiker's responsibility to make sure, if at all possible, *not* to get into a situation where you have to call rangers to come and get you, because you have now endangered them as well. Obviously, this is not always possible," is the important lesson I want to recite, but I just sigh and settle for knowing that Soho is OK.

Relieved that all members of the Moving Village are safe and accounted for, I reflect on the experience. It was scary but thrilling—more so now that I have come out of it in one piece. I didn't expect to be hiking in a blizzard in the middle of spring, but the weather is unpredictable up in these mountains, and it's best to be prepared. It also helps to be part of a village when snowmageddon strikes.

CHAPTER 14

Not the End

THE KID HAS BEEN HIKING WITH A LARGE STICK THAT HE FOUND DURING his first week on the trail. I'm not sure how he does it. I personally don't think I would have made it this far without my trekking poles. My poles are sort of an extension of my arms: They help make descents easier on my knees; they keep me balanced; and they take some of the load, transferring weight from my pack off of my back.

I once tested myself by trying to hike up and down a mountain without my trekking poles. Bad move. I tripped and almost head-butted a tree. At this point, it has become unnatural for me *not* to use my poles. Like a motorcycle without a kickstand, I fall over without them. OK, maybe not that extreme, but I do feel more in control when I'm using them. The Kid, on the other hand, makes it look easy to hike with nothing but a stick held loosely in one hand like a biblical Moses.

Each hiker from the Moving Village has carved his or her trail name on the Kid's walking staff. Recently I was told that hiking groups on the Appalachian Trail do not last long together. Resistant, I felt certain that rule did not apply to the Moving Village. The affection I feel for my trail family has ignited my hope of a Katahdin Moving Village summit. I imagine us crowding around the famous wooden sign for a final group photo. Before long, though, our group shrinks to only four hikers: Overdrive, Big Foot, Soho, and me.

Last month Tower and Doc started to hike farther than the rest of us, which put them days ahead. That still left the Moving Village eight strong until the Kid went missing a few days ago. Through Facebook, he was found back in his hometown. In hindsight, we should have known. He was way underprepared for a long-distance hiker. He didn't have a mini stove, and he only carried a day pack, which is not sufficient for someone planning to live out here for several months. In fact, I don't recall him ever saying he was going to hike all the way to Maine. My conclusion is that his intention was to come out here for a few days or a few weeks of hiking and that was it.

When the Moving Village stayed an extra night at Kincora Hostel and Overdrive and I hiked on ahead, I began to sense that my time with the group was coming to an end. We found it difficult to understand why, just two days after we had gone into town for rest, laundry, and a shower, the Moving Village wanted to rest, do laundry, and shower again. Sure, I like to stay fresh and fabulous, but I also want to make a serious effort to keep moving. As it turned out, the Moving Village slackpacked and did nearly the same miles as Overdrive and I.

I'm not a proponent of slackpacking, which means hiking without your backpack while someone transports it to your next stop. It just doesn't coincide with my idea of a thru-hike. For me, this journey is not about the miles, but the act of moving forward while carrying everything I need to live on. It's not about getting to the end but the process it takes to get there. It's the sense of strength, endurance, and accomplishment that makes this experience worthwhile.

With that said, each person hikes the Appalachian Trail in his or her own way, and for his or her own reasons. There's no right or wrong way to do it. Be that as it may, when I encounter Big Foot hiking toward me with a pink day pack that a 5-year-old girl would wear to her kindergarten class, I can't help but feel as if my slackpacking friends are missing the point of this whole hiking adventure. Then again, who am I to set the standard in AT thru-hiking? Although, I must admit, Big Foot's flowery kiddie bag does little to diminish his giant stature. The guy is still a Frankenstein.

He laughs at my jest and echoes the *loser* name I give them.

"Slackpack is whack," I taunt as I watch them hike—or more like skip— along the trail Overdrive and I just came from.

"Look at them, Overdrive. They look like jolly Smurfs."

I turn back around with my heavy-ass pack, wishing I were slackpacking. When I see them days later, I find out that they slackpacked for the benefit of the three hikers who are in pain due to injuries. Jolly 3-0 is struggling with his shoulder, and Halfway's knee is getting worse. At Marion, Virginia, they both went to a hospital and were told they needed to rest. Sadly, Halfway announces she is leaving the trail and going back home to Germany. Jolly expresses his desire to slackpack the rest of the AT after a short break from the trail, but in all honesty, it looks like this is the end for him as well. With a bad knee, Downhill barely makes it to camp today. As I hike behind him, I can see how agonizing each step is for him. I want to take some of the pain from him and carry it with me, like everyone did with Halfway's gear when her knee was bothering her during our first week on the trail. I know that Downhill's hike is done for when he says he feels pain going down a hill and none going up.

"We may have to change your name to *Uphill*," Overdrive says.

———————

It's a rainy morning at Chestnut Knob Shelter. Big Foot, Soho, Downhill, and Overdrive have begun their hike. I'm not keen on starting my hike in the rain, so I sit eating oatmeal and drinking coffee at a picnic table situated in a shelter with a closed door that is failing to keep out the chill.

As I relax in a morning daze, I turn to a sudden slapping sound coming from a hiker called Provisions, whose actions contradict his trail name. Hiker rumor on the trail has it that he has been at this shelter for over a week, bumming food from every hiker who walks through the shelter door. He offered me a dollar for any food I could spare for breakfast. I gave him a packet of crackers without taking his bill. It's the least I could do for a fellow thru-hiker. Turns out he asked Overdrive for food as well, which is how I found out about his long stay at the shelter and his panhandling schemes.

Provisions, like hell. His name should be Little Possessions, Poorly Prepared, Little to Nothing, Ain't Got Crap.

Last night while we tried to eat dinner, he insisted on demonstrating how he would defend himself against a bear attack. Loud unexpected karate/kung fu shouts were part of his demonstration. If he weren't so serious about each move, I would have laughed out loud.

"You want to hold your position," he continued. "Let them know you are in charge. Your fingers are powerful weapons. You go for the eyes, like this . . . KIIIAA!"

I tried to ignore him but found it difficult when another "KIIIAA" startled me to attention.

"What the . . . ? I think I just peed myself," I whispered to a hiker who was sitting next to me at the table.

Now I turn toward where the slapping sound is coming from and see Provisions flogging himself with a scourge he made out of thick rope. The action is monk-like.

I wonder where his hair shirt is?

I glance at Peach—named thus because she bruises easily like a peach, not because she has peach fuzz, as I tease. She's the only other hiker in the shelter, and we share a wide-eyed look. I hope she stays close, just in case. Still, I'm a little curious. I want to ask Provisions if he's repenting for some sin, and if so, is it murder?

Before I get a chance, he says, "I whip my back every morning," to no one in particular. "It revives my skin and wakes me up."

"Oh, OK, um, coffee does that for me," I say, hoping he doesn't whip me for that comment.

Peach gives a chuckle, and I'm glad she does, because it lightens the air of the heavy weirdness this guy is emitting.

I finish my breakfast faster than usual and gather my gear. Then I dart out before Provisions threatens to wake me with his whip or offers to teach me some more defensive moves against creatures that can rip me in half with a swipe of their sharp claws.

We're now leaving Bland, Virginia, where we had our last night together as the Moving Village. Halfway, Jolly 3-0, Downhill, and Big Foot's parents are driving Soho, Big Foot, Overdrive, and me to the trailhead to see us off. It's a melancholy trip. Halfway is going over photos on her camera, reminiscing with Soho; this seems to be her way of soothing Soho's sadness. The rest of us sit quietly. I stare out the window and wonder if I'll ever see Jolly, the army hero, again; or Downhill, with his childlike humor; or Halfway, with her funny way of saying English words. She makes me laugh the most, and I will miss her dearly.

At the trailhead, we're slow to part. Sorrowful hearts find it hard to say goodbye. Timers on cameras are set to take final group photos. I'm not good with goodbyes, but who is? Nonetheless, Halfway and Soho are having the hardest time. I walk away when they sobbingly embrace each other. The grief cuts deep enough for me that I don't want to add to it by watching their struggle with separation.

Our farewell takes longer than I wish it would. I want to get going and leave the gloom behind. But when the SUV pulls off with part of my trail family, I don't move until it disappears completely around a turn.

"Oh, well," are Big Foot's words of woe about our group becoming only four hikers. Simple, yet clear that life goes on.

That part of my hike is over. Almost 600 miles with the best company I could ever want to be left in the woods with. It's now time to move on without them. I still have more than 1,500 miles to go and much more to experience. Overdrive leads the way, then Big Foot. I take the rear with a dispirited Soho. I want to say the right words to make it all better for her, but I have none to give. I grab her hand for comfort's sake. She squeezes tight and says she's OK before letting go. We follow along quietly until . . . .

"What kind of crazy-looking contraption are you wearing, Biggie?" I say to Big Foot, pointing at what resembles a tennis visor transplanted onto a safari hat.

"It was a gift. I had to accept it," he says.

He takes it off, gives it a quick look, and then puts it back on. The sight is too much to pass up.

"Hold on, let me take a picture," I say, grabbing for my camera.

"Oh, no, you don't. We don't need evidence of this. I'm leaving it at the next shelter," he says adamantly.

"Why? It looks adorable. Don't you think, Soho?" I ask, teasing.

"Yeah, if he was a giant clown," she says, laughing for the first time in days.

"It's definitely an eye-catcher," I add, as we all laugh.

Over the next few days, the four of us begin to part ways; after only doing 3 miles from the last shelter, a disheartened Soho stays at Woods Hole Hostel. Overdrive moves ahead, as usual, and Big Foot and I decide to ease our minds with jokes while we hike. The rest of the day is free of worries and full of laughter.

My last few days with Big Foot are enjoyable, but the final few miles are rough and rocky, which slows us down. We eventually make it to a garage hostel called Four Pines, where Overdrive is waiting for us with beer and burgers on a grill (a veggie burger for me). We laugh and eat until the arrival of darkness brings weariness.

As we retire for the night, a feeling of sorrow that I kept at bay during the day returns. I try to ease my mind with thoughts of how far I've come for a novice hiker. At this point in my trek, I'm feeling better than ever about completing this thru-hike. With a tired smile—tired from more than simply hiking, I'm mentally drained—I drift into a deep sleep.

The next day Overdrive and I say our farewells to Big Foot, who is doing a zero at Four Pines Hostel. We hop into the back of a truck driven by Joe, the owner of the hostel. We join Peach and a couple of other hikers for the ride back to Damascus, Virginia, where we will attend a weekend-long hiker festival called Trail Days. Overdrive and I also plan to sign up for Bob Peoples' Hard Core crew for two days of trail maintenance. I estimate that Big Foot will be 100 miles ahead of Overdrive and me when we return to the trail. Although it will take a major push to catch up to the big lug, if we put it in over-overdrive, we can make it happen.

Big Foot waves goodbye as we pull away from the hostel.

Damn, I miss him already.

This is the end of the Moving Village—and the beginning of an all-new hike. Change can be frightening at times, but out here it's our way of life. When I stepped onto the AT, I sought change. I wanted to move away from a static existence. Suitably, the end of one thing opens the way for something wondrous. I see not the end but a new start.

Part 3

MR. FABULOUS

CHAPTER 15

A Series of Fortunate Events

"I buried it in a sandwich bag full of rice," I explain to Deerpath. "Someone told me that soaks up the water."

My camera may be dry, but it still doesn't work. Apparently snapping pictures in the rain isn't good for it. *Who knew?*

This is the second camera I roughed up on the trail. The first one I sat on too many times, causing the lens to no longer extend. Now I'm in need of another one, and Deerpath is kind enough to drive Peach, Overdrive, and I to the nearest shopping center so I can purchase a third camera to destroy. My goal has been to make it to Katahdin in one piece, but I guess I should have included my camera in that plan. This time I add an extended warranty since I seem to go through cameras like thru-hikers go through boots.

I met Deerpath during my first week on the Appalachian Trail. He introduced me to banana chips dipped in peanut butter, a perfect delicacy for my sophisticated hiker appetite.

We're all here in Damascus, Virginia, for Trail Days, an Appalachian Trail festival where past, present, and aspiring thru-hikers, along with hiking enthusiasts, gather and celebrate the love of hiking.

Damascus is known as Trail Town USA because of all the trails that run through it, including the Appalachian Trail, the Iron Mountain Trail, the Virginia Creeper Trail, and US Bicycle Route 76. It's one of the most hiker-friendly towns in America, something I can attest to from my stay a few weeks back. It's by far the best place to host the largest gathering of AT hikers, one of the reasons I took a ride back here.

The festivities include a parade, movies, lectures, slide shows, outdoor concerts, and a hiker talent show. When Overdrive, Peach, and I arrived yesterday afternoon, we went straight to a free hiker feed at the First Baptist

Church. Volunteers served burgers and hotdogs, but I stuck with fruit, potato chips, and a soda. One of the nice ladies serving the food discovered that I'm a vegetarian and brought over a few slices of cheese for me.

What, no wine to go with it? I wanted to joke, but I graciously thanked her instead.

"They have free showers here tomorrow morning," said Peach, pointing at a disaster relief trailer not far from us.

"Whoa," I said, nearly choking on the cheese. "Showers? I feel so loved."

Free food and showers is definitely the way to a thru-hiker's heart.

Now, we head to the small town's park to check out the vendors' offerings and enter our names in raffles for free hiking gear.

"Hey, I hear that the First Baptist Church is offering free foot massages," says Overdrive.

"Then let's go! My feet can use some caring attention." I joyfully skip ahead but almost trip over my *chancletas*. (Chancletas is a Spanish word for flip-flops, which Overdrive pronounces *chunk-lettuce*. His mouth is not made for Spanish words.)

Later in the evening, I head over to the Trail Days campground and what has come to be known as Tent City. Joe, the owner of the Four Pines Hostel, has set up a pavilion with a grill for whomever wants to stop by for food and conversation.

All day, his 12-year-old son, Josh, has been in and out of the nearby tent-filled woods. It's nearly 9 P.M., and I'm ready to see what the hoopla is all about.

"It's dark, but I know where to go," Josh says.

"Are you sure? Should I bring bear mace?" I jest.

"Nah, it's safe," he assures me.

"Oh, OK, then," I say as I follow the kid into the woods.

"Bring my son back alive, Mr. Fabulous," says Josh's dad.

"I will, sir. I'll protect him with my life—as soon as I make sure I'm OK," I say. We move into the dark woods, where a different breed of wild creature is partying and doing who knows what.

"Stay close, kid," I say to the eager tween.

"Come on, then," he replies, running ahead.

We hear sounds coming from various places in the darkness where the trail splits off into different camping areas. Josh claims to have the best spot picked out for me. Our headlamps light the trail, but distant faces are hard to distinguish. Two hikers I think I know hand me a concoction that I don't question but merely take a swig of.

When at Trail Days . . . .

We move deeper into the mazelike woods, taking paths that lead us to different campfires. Each one offers some form of show: One has a singer, another a juggler, a few have guitar players. At others, hikers just stand around feeding the fire, and at one campfire a drunken storyteller holds forth. Although his delivery is altered by one too many beers, his performance is worth staying for.

Dark figures walk toward me. I strain to see faces I don't recognize.

Did I think I knew every AT hiker? Of course not.

Josh leads me even farther into the woods.

"We're almost there," he says.

"There? Where?"

"Come on!"

We get to an area with a big, lit-up dome structure floating several feet high and resembling something out of a Cirque du Soleil set.

"This is the entrance to the madness," says my little guide.

"Madness? You didn't say anything about madness," I joke.

Caution pinches me, but curiosity shoos it away as we walk under the dome to a large opening just outside the woods.

"Come on. There's a big bonfire this way," says my young guide.

He's right. There is a good-size bonfire lighting the faces of hikers who gather in small groups around it. Large logs are set close to the blaze for seating. Hikers are anticipating some form of entertainment; a band is the rumor. On the opposite side of the fire, a girl moves her hips, skillfully keeping two hula hoops twirling around her body. Her movements resemble those of a swimmer underwater. I can't tear my eyes away. It's hypnotizing.

"Mr. Fabulous!"

Startled, I swing my arms around as if waving away a swarm of bees.

It's Steps, who has popped out of the crowd like a wildlife television host in pursuit of a dangerous animal. Wide-eyed, she looks to her left, then to her right, and storms off without another word.

"Hey, kid," I say, "whatever that girl is having, I want to stay clear of."

She's clearly having fun, but I'm not sure if she's drunk, high, or just being Steps.

"That girl is strange; I think I love her," I joke to a passing hiker.

More cups of cocktails are passed around. There's music, people dancing, a juggler, and another hula-hooper. A couple on a log furiously make out. *Get a tent!* Two hikers pretend box then wrestle to the ground. I pass a hiker giving a speech to others about toxic additives in our food and drinks. He pauses occasionally to take a swig of his cup filled with the unknown concoction.

I don't want the night to end, but by 2 A.M., a yawn shifts my mind into a lethargic state. It's way past my hiker bedtime, and after a day filled with activities, I'm fading fast. I get Josh safely back to his dad before heading to my tent, which is pitched in the yard of a restaurant owned by a man we befriended during our hike through town a few weeks ago.

However long I sleep, it's not long enough. Overdrive wakes me, and we head to the First Baptist Church for free internet. This has to be the most I've ever been to church since I was a child. I wonder if this is their ploy to convert me, because if it is, it's working.

The volunteers are as nice and as wonderful as can be—and I'm not just saying that because they're catering to all of my hiker needs.

Hmm . . . yeah, maybe that is the reason.

Afterward we head over to hear Jennifer Pharr Davis, the newly crowned fastest Appalachian Trail thru-hiker, give a presentation about her feat and her book. She thru-hiked the AT in 46 days, 11 hours, and 20 minutes. *Ouch!* The thought alone gives me cramps.

I'm walking through the gravel main parking area full of vendors when I hear, "Mr. Fabulous!"

I turn to see a tall, burly man wave me down. He is standing behind a long table in a footwear vendor pavilion. I don't recognize him, but he somehow knows me.

"Can I touch your dreads?" It's such an odd question coming from this tough-looking man. I don't think I'll ever be comfortable with people asking me that.

Years ago, I was at a bar in the Chelsea area of New York City, and while I was talking to a friend, I felt my hair being tugged. I turned around and saw

one of my dreads in a man's mouth, like a rose in the mouth of someone dancing the tango. He batted his eyelashes at me and smiled as if to say, "Come
and get me." Now, first of all, that was *nasty*. I mean my hair was clean, but
he didn't know that, and *damn*, what if he didn't brush his teeth that day? My
dreads could have gotten gingivitis.

Since then, I've been wary of people touching my hair, and at this
moment, I have an uninvited vision of my dreads in the guy's mouth. I wish
to convey to this large man that under no circumstances will I permit my hair
to be eaten, but instead I say, "Sure." *What am I supposed to say?*

It's beyond me how some strangers will touch my hair upon meeting me
for the first time instead of going for a traditional handshake. I've had people
stroke my dreadlocks as if petting a cat. They're oblivious that touching a
person's hair is an intimate act. It's the same reason why I don't go around
caressing a beautiful woman's face. Even if I politely asked, "Pardon, may I
touch your skin?" it's a move that would, no doubt, get me arrested.

So, now I'm standing still as this large man runs his fingers through several locks when I only agreed to one.

OK, feeling awkward . . . .

Should I be flattered that my dreadlocks are drawing positive attention?
Maybe. I'll take peace over war anytime, but still, a high-five would have
been preferable.

I head over to the hiker parade that is now in progress.

"Why aren't you marching in the parade?" Steps asks me, as I walk along
a safe distance from the water fight that has broken out.

"Oh, Mr. Fabulous can't get his dreadlocks wet," I say, in my best snob-
bish tone.

I've been ducking water balloons since the start of this hiker march and
I'm safe until Overdrive sprays me with his water gun.

What the hell! He's supposed to be my thru-brotha.

"Dude, I'm going to shove that water gun so far up your *arse* that you're
going to drown. Now cut it out," I say to him.

I turn away only to get his wet response on my back. "I'm going to . . . ."
I grab for his shooter and get another wet shot before he quickly runs off.

"Grow up!" I yell after him.

What is this tradition of soaking hikers? Did it begin at the first parade
when an onlooker yelled, "Hey hiker trash, you smell," and chucked a bucket

of water onto a thru-hiker? Or did it start as a way for hikers to keep cool on a hot summer day? No matter the origin, it's easy to get caught up in a battle of harmless water fun, even if you're trying to stay dry.

The talent show at the town's gazebo stage showcases many gifted performers—and some not so gifted, which makes it that much more entertaining. Only thru-hikers can participate. There's devil stick juggling and another hula hoop act, as well as a fire-breathing act and a bluegrass band.

I leave before the winners are announced to pick up my boots at a vendor who offered to seal the worn-out front soles. On my way there, I see the big touchy-feely guy walking toward me.

OK, my dreads are off limits.

"Hey, Mr. Fabulous," he says as we shake hands.

He looks me straight in the eyes. "This will be the last time I see you," he says, "so I'll leave you with these words: Be kind to all, don't take your friends for granted, and be memorable."

Huh?

I'm taken aback to hear these wise words coming from a large guy who looks like he owns a seedy tattoo shop next to a biker bar. He speaks not just with his voice but also with his handshake, his eyes, and an energy that envelops me from head to toe.

Who is this guy, and why do I want him to touch my hair again?

"Wow, that's deep. I wish everyone's farewell was as elegant as yours. You're a good man. Thank you," is what I want to say, but I'm only able to garble a few words. I may have thanked him, but I'm not sure.

We then go our separate ways. I'm rarely speechless, but this man's words are worth being silent for. I look back to see if he has wings to take him back to that mountain of wisdom he flew down from. No wings, but I half expect him to disappear, so I stand there watching him walk away until I can barely see him.

This journey is something else.

A few weeks back, the first time we were in Damascus, I had another encounter that changed the way I think about my journey.

"Hey, can I take a picture of you?" a voice said from behind me.

I turned to see a thru-hiker with a large white beard that gave him a garden gnome look.

"Sure! I love posing for photos," I said gleefully.

He introduced himself as Birdman, took the picture, and then handed Overdrive the camera so he could take a photo of the two of us together.

"I take pictures of hikers I meet," said Birdman.

He continued to explain: "A few weeks back, I met someone who hiked the AT last year, and I asked him if there was anything he would have done differently. Without hesitating, he said that he took many wonderful photos of scenery, but wished he had taken more of the people he met. A large part of this experience has to do with the people."

And just like that, this gentle person gave me advice I would adhere to through the rest of my journey. It instantly made sense to me. I can take pictures of mountains, of breathtaking views, of all the beauty the Appalachian Trail possesses and end up with a few stunning photos. But pictures of people I meet along the trail can evoke a memory of kind words, a shared experience. It's the people that make this trail truly special.

"That's a great idea. I'm going to start by taking your photo, Birdman," I said, knowing this photo will remind me of that moment and its lesson.

Although I didn't see Birdman for Trail Days, I can't help but connect him with this small town. The jolly photo I took of him reminds me of his kindness and his eagerness to relate to others. It's what I aim to do out here on the AT.

My hopes were high when I returned to this town, and it has not let me down. Trail Days is a gathering of open-minded people who come to celebrate life in their own way and to embrace the now. With a series of fortunate events and encounters, this festival has reconnected me with my fellow hikers, introduced me to new ones, and brought me closer to others—and not just because one of them touched my hair.

CHAPTER 16

Peace, Love & All That Good Stuff!

I MIGHT NOT KNOW WHERE I AM . . . BUT I AIN'T LOST!!, SAYS A BUMPER sticker on the Four Pines Hostel bulletin board. The board displays summit postcards, thank-you notes, and stickers with quotes like the one I just read.

The saying rings true to me. Some may find themselves turned around on the Appalachian Trail, but there is one sure thing: As long as you're on the AT, you will eventually find your way via the white blaze.

This goes right along with the motto I use when I go astray, not just out here but in life generally: *I'm not lost . . . I'm just misplaced*. It's a somewhat comforting perspective that I take, knowing that I will eventually correct my course whenever I temporarily lose my way.

If you lose that white blaze, however, then kiss your keister goodbye, says my inner sarcastic voice.

Instead of hiking on, Overdrive and I took yesterday's rain as a reason to stay at Four Pines Hostel in Catawba, Virginia. Hikers looking for a place to settle for the night joined us at the large garage turned hostel. Overdrive and I met thru-hikers who had been traveling several days behind us on the trail. Because we backtracked to Damascus for Trail Days and then volunteered for the Hard Core trail crew, we missed five days of hiking, and we're now surrounded by a new circle of unfamiliar thru-hikers.

With each new face, I have come to visualize the process of thru-hiking as a whirlwind. We spin forward along the trail with other hikers for a while; then eventually we each spin away from the circle, shooting every which way. Some move ahead, others go into town for a zero or resupply, and many simply hike at their own pace. Different hikers get sucked into the eye of the storm and then spiral their own way as the whirlwind moves on.

With a heavy heart, I realize this is actually the first time I'm hiking without a familiar group. It's a whole new thru-hike with an all-new breed of hikers. Seeing different faces, well, I'm down with that, and change is inevitable, but part of me is longing to be back in the circle I've been swirling in for the last two months. I make up my mind that I'm going to catch up to Big Foot and Soho as soon as possible.

"Mr. Fabulous, I'm glad to finally meet you," says a hiker after I introduce myself to her as she walks into the hostel, ending her day of hiking. "I've been following your shelter posts for a while."

Really?

I enjoy reading entries in the registers, and there are a few people whose comments I look forward to reading, but it didn't occur to me that anyone would be following my entries.

"Your closing statement is awesome," she adds.

"Oh—*Peace, Love & All That Good Stuff.* Thanks," I say, thrilled.

Just before I began my thru-hike in March, I decided a positive approach would serve me well during my quest into the unknown. I figured my mind would be my biggest strength out here, and if times looked bleak or a bit unbearable, I could use some sort of mantra to lead me out of it—some feel-good message I could follow and share with others. *Peace, Love & All That Good Stuff* is what I came up with. It makes me smile every time I write the words in a shelter log. For me it has become more than some catchphrase. It's how I approach each and every day out here. With that attitude, I've enjoyed and embraced—or at least accepted—just about everything this unpredictable trail has thrown my way.

"I'm so glad you like it," I add.

Then it hits me: If others are reading my post, I need to be clever and wise with my entries.

Oh, the pressure . . . .

CHAPTER 17

A Suspicious Mind

BEING A NEW YORKER MAKES ME SUSPICIOUS OF THE KINDNESS OF strangers, and this trail is full of suspects. Locals who live along the Appalachian Trail leave food and drinks at trailheads, offer showers and shelter at their homes, and ask for nothing in return. To me, that is mind-blowing. They're not selling candy bars to raise money for a fictitious basketball team, like the kids in New York City subways, when what they really want is cash for a new pair of Jordans.

New Yorkers don't take anything from strangers, unless they plan on handing over some money in return. Avoiding eye contact is a must; if you don't, strangers will latch onto that look like a tick on dreadlocks.

I think back to when I first heard of trail angels.

Who are they? Why do they do what they do? Why would someone leave treats on the side of the trail?

I'm bewildered as I stare down at an apple pie with a note that says, *Take a piece. You deserve it . . . you're a thru-hiker.*

If I ever came across a baked good on a sidewalk before thru-hiking the AT, I would simply stroll right past it, assuming it was trash.

To be clear, I do believe most humans are good and are capable of kindness, but for someone who doesn't even know me to suddenly give me a gift? Surely there's a catch.

"Hello, sir. May I interest you in a free phone with a contract of only twenty-four months?" I'm asked somewhere in midtown Manhattan.

"Sorry, I already have a phone," I respond, and then notice: "Wait, is that a flip phone with a pullout antenna? Do they still make that 1996 antique? You can't give them away," I continue, astonished.

"OK . . . have a good day, sir," he says as he carries his bag of worthless phones as far away from me as possible.

Nothing is given for free, and if it is, it's a crap deal.

Through the years and almost on a daily basis, I've seen the sharks preying on the streets in search of fresh blood. Since by now I'm incapable of falling for their hustle, the schemers of the city have adjusted their strategy to win over people like me by presenting . . . alluring women.

A few years back, I was enjoying a lovely summer day at Bryant Park in New York City. I didn't have anywhere in particular to be, so I was relaxing with a book. I must add that I was feeling exceptionally good-looking. We all have days like this, and on this day everything was on point. I had just shaved, my dreadlocks were twisted nicely, and I was wearing a new pair of jeans with the poise of a model. I was full—not of myself, although it may sound that way—but of a self-confidence that was a product of a perfect, harmonious day.

So I wasn't surprised when a lovely woman excused herself and expressed admiration for my hair.

"Why thank you," I said modestly, or at least that's the way I meant it to come across.

She asked if she could join me at the small lawn table I was chillin' at.

"Oh, of course," I replied, with some charm, or at least that's the way I meant it to come across.

She went on about how she was drawn to men with dreadlocks. I searched for a reason to stand up so she could see how my jeans really accentuated my figure, but before I got a chance, I heard, "Hey, I'm John."

I was so taken by the way this seductress was speaking to me that I didn't see the male adolescent standing behind her.

"Oh, hey, John. I'm Derick," I responded, suspiciously shaking his outstretched hand.

"So, we are from the Church of blah blah blah . . . " he began.

I stopped listening after *Church*. Not that I'm against anything that gives people peace for their soul and self, but I'm not a fan of suddenly springing an attack on the spirit using sex appeal as bait.

Thou shall not use physical attraction to tempt and then preach.

I realize that not all encounters with strangers are dishonest. But these are only brief examples of the encounters in my life that have crafted my suspicious mind. So forgive me if I'm a bit taken aback on the AT, where I find myself surrounded by unreserved affection with seemingly no hidden agendas. I'm beginning to realize that the rules of humankind are different out here. In fact, the instant I stepped foot on the AT, my perception began a slow conversion from doubt to belief. Belief that not all strangers are schemers, that a gift from an unknown person can be just that, *a gift*, not some covert plan to separate me from my possessions.

Besides, what could anyone swindle from me out here? The possessions I am carrying are of little value to anyone but myself. So, with that in mind, I decide to put my paranoia in check. I can trust that the sugar powder currently covering my face (from the doughnut I inhaled after finding it in a cooler left on a trailhead) does not come with a price. It is absolutely *free*— money free, tax free. Not gluten free, but I can live with that.

I now wonder how I can bottle this outflow of generosity and bring it out into the real world. Or *is* the AT the real world? If it isn't, it should be. It has taken some time, but I've stopped questioning why strangers embrace us like close friends and leave trail magic for thru-hikers. Now my question is: Why can't the rest of the world follow suit?

CHAPTER 18

The Honeymoon Hikers

I STARTED OUT TODAY THINKING I WOULD HIKE 22 MILES, BUT I'VE BEEN moving at a slow pace—like someone strolling through a park aimlessly chasing butterflies. Subconsciously, 22 miles is a goal I don't take seriously. Ten miles seems like all I have in me. Hope of catching up to Big Foot with a week of power hiking begins to fade.

Damn, I wish he would slow down. He didn't do big miles when he was with the Moving Village.

I text Overdrive to let him know I won't be seeing him this evening. He in turn informs me that he saw the Honeymoon Hikers here in Daleville, Virginia, and that they're staying at an inn for the night. I decide to head over and say hello to my favorite couple on the trail.

I first met Ratman and Tumbler, the Honeymoon Hikers, when I was still with the Moving Village. We were in Hot Springs, North Carolina, and it was Ratman's birthday. His son came to visit with a cake and some cherry moonshine that Ratman's dad had made. The *shine,* as Ratman calls it, went down smoother than I'd imagined moonshine would. I recall a memory of my grandfather making Ron Caña, a Puerto Rican version of moonshine. With a smirk, he once offered me a sip. Just before I placed the glass to my lips, my inner voice shouted out a warning, but like always, I ignored it. Before I even finished a swallow, the gift of breathing was ripped from me as I felt myself drowning in liquid fire. I swung my arms as if trying to swim up to surface for air. Through tears I saw my grandfather with an arrogant look on his face, as if to say, *Yeah, you have to be a real macho to drink this.* I tried to man up and not look like a lightweight, but when there's very little oxygen entering your body, it's hard to play it cool. He offered me another sip, but I waved it away as I leaned on a wall, like a boxer on the ropes about to go down for the count. Thanks to the crazy old man, I'm pretty sure I have a permanent scar in my throat caused by that homemade poison.

But drinking Ratman's *cherry-liciousness* was more to my liking, and it solidified my friendship with the Honeymoon Hikers.

It was a rainy and gloomy day when I first found myself hiking with the Honeymoon Hikers. Ratman's stories about the trail magic they'd received diverted my attention from the wet clothes that sat heavily on me as the rain kept coming down.

"...and there was this guy that picked us up at Davenport Gap. He took us to his store, gave us a free resupply, fed us at a Subway, took us home for the night, and bought us breakfast before driving us back to the trailhead the next morning."

"Whaaa, that's some trail magic!" I exclaimed.

"Yeah, we've been blessed," said Ratman.

That was a few weeks ago, and now I head over to the inn for a quick visit with the Honeymoon Hikers. But when I arrive at the inn and approach the front desk, it dawns on me: I don't know their real names.

"Hi, um, I know this is going to sound weird, but you see, I'm thru-hiking, and I just found out there's a thru-hiker couple staying here, but I only know them by their trail name, the Honeymoon Hikers. Ring a bell?" I ask with little hope.

The girl at the counter smiles with a knowing look.

"What do they look like?" she asks politely.

"Like hiker trash," I say, chuckling, then clear my throat when I don't get a laugh. ""Ahem. Well, the guy is bald with a gray beard, and his wife is feminine but strong, like she can lift 200 pounds and kick some butt. They're wearing matching black T-shirts that read, 'This walk is for Jesus because He made THE WALK for me,' but it's a bit faded and missing letters, so it may look more like 'is alk o J be He mad HE ALK or me.' Her shirt sleeves are cut off because she's cock diesel, like Wonder Woman. Oh, and they have a Southern twang. Sound familiar?"

The girl behind the counter looks over at her coworker and asks, "Did you check in a couple like that?"

"I don't think so. I'm sure I would remember such a couple."

"Yeah, me too. They may have checked in before we started our shift," she says, scanning over a check-in list. "There are only a few couples here. Let me see if I can narrow it down."

Hikers pass me, and although I don't recognize them, I know they're thru-hikers; it's something we all sense from each other. I figure it's infamous body odor that offends unaware civilians but somehow unites thru-hikers.

"Hey, do you guys know the Honeymoon Hikers?" I ask.

They don't, but a hiker just walking in says he saw them enter a room on the same floor as his. The girl at the counter overhears and quickly figures it out. She picks up a phone and dials a room number.

"Hi, is this the Honeymoon Hikers?" she asks without hesitation. "OK great, there's a . . . ."

"Mr. Fabulous," I say with a smile.

She laughs. "Mr. Fabulous is here to see you . . . OK . . . bye." She hangs up. "They're on their way down."

Within minutes, the Honeymoon Hikers walk through the lobby doors looking showered and refreshed.

Oh, how I wish to be that right now.

And although they're clean and I'm less than, they still give me a hug. It feels good to see these two again.

We talk a while before I notice the time. "It's 5 P.M. I should get going."

"Why? We have an extra bed. You can stay with us," says Tumbler.

I think it through. I'm tired, and the 5 miles to the next shelter seems too far for me now.

"Why am I thinking about it? Yes, please, thank you, love you."

"You know about the hiker feed this weekend, right?" Ratman asks as we walk to their room. One of the many interesting things about this couple is that because they've already completed an AT thru-hike in the past, they know every highlight of this adventure, whether it's a hiker feed, a bargain hostel, or the best place to eat in town. If there is trail magic in the state where they're hiking, they'll sniff it out. They're a better source of information than some guidebooks in that respect.

"No, I didn't hear about it," I respond.

"It's at Blue Ridge Parkway, near Thunder Hill Shelter," Tumbler says.

"Guess I know where I'll be this weekend!"

Pizza, shower, and bed—now this is trail magic heaven! "I have intimate love for you, Mr. Fabulous," were a sauced hiker's last words to me as I helped him get safely to a hostel a few months ago. Back then, I was surprised by those words. But at this moment, I want to express my eternal thanks for the kindness the Honeymoon Hikers have shown me. Like my inebriated hiker buddy, I want to say that I have *intimate love* for them. It seems to be the only way to express my appreciation. It's one thing hearing it from an intoxicated person outside in the open, however, and another thing entirely coming from me in the confines of a small hotel room. So I decide against the idea of sharing my affection. Instead I reach for another slice of pizza and hope my new roommates don't snore.

CHAPTER 19

Food for the Soul

By 7 a.m. Ratman, Tumbler, and I are ready to do some serious miles. My intent today is to make up for yesterday's lax hike, and the Honeymoon Hikers are set on making it to the hiker feed this weekend.

Hmm. Calculated trail magic.

I chuckle at the thought, but by midday I find nothing humorous about our vigorous hike.

"Ratman, let's break," I plead as I struggle to keep in step with him.

We've been hiking nonstop at a demanding pace for an hour, and I'm depleted of nearly all of my mental and physical resources.

"OK, two minutes," says Ratman, the AT drill sergeant.

"Two . . . minu—oka—," I breathlessly whisper.

I drop my pack and then sit on it; Ratman keeps his on. Within seconds he's ready to get going again. Looking up at the evil half of the Honeymoon pair, I whimper, "I think I hate you."

He laughs at my suffering.

"Now you know what I go through," says Tumbler, who has taken off her pack as well.

"She gets on me for timing our breaks," he says with a smile.

OK, I'm going to have to be smart about this. Ratman likes to talk as much as I do—I wonder if I can trick him into breaking longer?

"Ratman, can you tell me how you and Tumbler met? And give me the long version."

"Yeah, I met her when I was doing time in prison, and she came to visit her husband. Now let's go!" he says, seeing right through my antics.

I'm fatigued and too exasperated to laugh, but the tiny bit of me that still has a sense of humor acknowledges that his response is funny. With a grunt,

I stand up, sling my pack over my back, and follow our relentless leader, with Tumbler close behind me.

We hike 28.2 miles, a record for both the Honeymoon Hikers and me. When we make it to Jennings Creek, Ratman does not waste any time getting us trail magic from a family camping there for the Memorial Day weekend. After eyeing a red cooler, he offers them a dollar for something to drink.

"No, that's not necessary," our new trail angel says, waving away the dollar. "We have more than enough drinks here for everyone."

Ratman glances at me with a *that's how you do it* look. I'm beginning to realize that the Honeymoon Hikers' gift for finding trail magic is more pre-planned than luck, a skill I'm learning from the masters. They're impressive at persuading strangers to happily offer trail magic without outright asking for it. AT hikers call this good-natured art *yogi-ing*. I watch with amusement at how they never ask for trail magic—that would come across as begging—but always seem to receive it.

"Sixty-three," is Ratman's response to my question about how much trail magic they have received thus far.

Ratman and Tumbler keep track of the trail magic they receive by writing, on a small pad, the place and the name of the trail angel, if they know it. Some trail magic appears by a trailhead with no sign of who left it.

"That includes rides into town and hiker feeds," he adds.

"Yeah, of course," I say, as if I have experienced such lavish gifts.

Sixty-three? What the heezel!

They definitely have a system working for themselves. In Brooklyn we would call them hustlers. But there's something about this couple that makes me want to offer them my life savings. They're sweet, funny, and they express kind words that always come across as genuine.

I have not received nearly as much trail magic as the Honeymoon Hikers have, but what little I have received has been memorable. It's not about the amount—I'm sure they feel the same way—but about timing. The most memorable trail magic has come when my food supply is low, or when I'm having a less than enjoyable hike.

"Guys, I can't believe we hiked 28 miles," I say as I plop myself down into my tent.

Ordinarily when I first arrive at camp, I like to fetch water and make dinner, but at this moment, I'm too frazzled to take another step.

"Twenty-eight point two! Don't rob us of the point two," corrects Tumbler.

"Ah, yes, lady. I think it was the point two that did me in." I don't have the strength to take my clothes off, blow up my air mattress, or roll out my sleeping bag. My body refuses to take any more orders from me. "Goodnight, guys. Hugs and kisses."

"Good night, Fabulous," I hear a distant voice say before slumber takes over. I lay my head down and instantly fall into a deep sleep.

I'm up by 6 a.m. and out with Ratman and Tumbler by 7. Sleeping with my hiking clothes on last night was not Fabulous-like, but it certainly made my morning preparations easy. Other than my tent, everything was still in my backpack.

"Let's get to this hiker feed," says Tumbler.

The plan is to hike thirteen miles to the annual Memorial Day weekend hiker feed at Thunder Hill.

Although I did a personal best of 28.2 miles yesterday, I feel surprisingly energetic. Still, I let the Honeymoon Hikers storm ahead as I steady my pace for a mellow day of hiking. By midday I reach a trailhead. On the side of the road, I see a note held down with a rock and the words *Hiker Feed* over an arrow pointing to the left. *I'm famished*—but shoot, when am I not? Hunger and mountains are a constant for us thru-hikers. I quickly turn left and walk toward some parked cars on the side of the road.

"*Woot woot,*" I call.

"*Woot woot,*" I hear in response.

The old Moving Village tally-ho is now used only by Overdrive and me.

"Mr. Fabulous!" I hear someone call.

I see Overdrive and a few hikers sitting on plastic lawn chairs as I approach a dirt lot.

"Hey, guys," I respond.

The hostesses of the hiker feed are three amiable ladies: Nancy, Lori, and Ann. I'm greeted, seated, and promptly served a plate of food.

"How do you keep your hands so clean?" asks Overdrive, who is watching me destroy my meal.

"Why wouldn't they be clean? I don't hike on my hands," I respond. "Are you digging for food out there?"

He smiles, stifling a laugh.

I look over at Ann, who perches on her lawn chair like a queen on her throne. She likes being around thru-hikers, and the more of us that arrive, the happier she seems.

"OK, what I have here are marbles," she says as she lifts up a clear ziplock bag full of marbles of various sizes and colors.

"I'd like for every one of you to take the one that calls you."

Great, extra weight, says the sarcastic voice in my head.

She asks us to take one marble and pass the bag around. I grab a purple one; I turn it around and see a dark shape resembling an eye. I grip it tight like a child holding on to a precious toy.

"OK, a few of you have heard this spiel, but for those of you who haven't . . . ."

Oh, no, here we go.

"You're probably wondering why we are doing this trail magic, what is our motivation," she continues.

I knew it. Another trap to convert us. Starving thru-hikers are such easy targets.

"This is not a religious sermon or anything like it. This is purely from our hearts."

OK . . . I'm listening.

"We trail angels feel honored to assist any hiker on their journey, whether they are section hikers or going the distance. Most people live in this world asleep. We go through our routines, have our habits, are seduced by the illusions of advertising and consumerism, which create a life lacking in authenticity and integrity and sometimes real love.

"You made a choice to leave this mundane world. You chose something so radically different that you had to view your life in a different way, even if it is only for a short time. Life gets simpler. You listen to your body when you are hungry, tired, or sore. You are more aware of your surroundings, more connected to nature. You are in tune with the rhythms of the seasons and weather. The pace allows you to see details some may not see in their lifetime.

"You are left to your thoughts without anything like television, videos, or computers to lull you into a brain-dead state. You visit shadows and pass doors to your history that you have tightly shut. If you are lucky, you get glimpses of your authentic self without judgment but with acceptance instead.

"You don't need as much. Your world is on your back. Relationships with other people have a different meaning. You realize you are in a big community where everyone is connected by the trail. You are willing to talk to strangers, ask for help, and provide help. You also provide opportunities for us, the mundane folks, to show our best, to be helping, giving, and compassionate. You allow us to resonate goodness in the world.

"All of this results in you learning more about who you are and what is important. When the individual human spirit grows, it impacts the world. The collective AT community helps to resonate a unique energy, a different way of being, and I can't help but think it has a ripple effect on the rest of the world. It is a chance for us to be roused from our sleep and see that we, too, can create a simpler, more compassionate, authentic life.

"The marble is a reminder that, at any moment, something wonderful can show up in your life. Whether it be a hiker feed, a cooler full of sodas, a much-needed ride to town, a lovely sunset, a profound conversation, or someone letting you use their shower. Mini miracles, magic, and unexpected gifts will come to you at the exact moment you need them. Let the marble help you remember that moment, and put energy into the marble every time magic happens. Then, on the days that are hard, pull out the marble and remember: Around the bend something is waiting for you. Have faith, soak up the energy you put in the marble, and move on."

Forget the extra weight—now I want another marble to carry with me.

Ann has just provided more nourishment for our psyche than all this food can supply for our bodies. She's given us nutrients for our souls. Her words remind us why we're out here. It's also a gratifying feeling to know the world acknowledges and respects us for our thru-hiking efforts.

My eyes start to well up, but I quickly compose myself. We all sit quietly for a moment, as if breaking the silence will break the spell she put us in.

When I feel the moment passing, I say to her, "Almost . . . you almost made me cry."

That makes way for a flow of conversation about what we just heard.

―――――――――

The allure of the Dutch Haus cabin, a bed and breakfast that caters to hikers during hiking season, in Montebello, Virginia, is too much for me to resist. While our laundry is being done, we hikers are given thick white robes to wear.

"Wooo, a robe, aren't we fancy?" I say as I feel the softness on my skin.

The aroma of food fills the air and stirs my stomach awake.

Oh, yeah. There's that hunger again.

The group of us are served lunch—for free—and we can leave afterward if we choose, but once we step into the cabin, receive the hospitality, and hear what is in store for dinner, we have to stay to experience everything the Dutch Haus has to offer. To up and leave would be like trying to take a small bite of a favorite dessert and throwing the rest away. *Not possible.*

After a night at the Dutch Haus, I am reluctant to let go of the comforts of this place. The first shuttle back to the trailhead leaves with Overdrive, Peach, and the Honeymoon Hikers. I promise to catch up, but deep inside, I sense the probability of that happening is pretty low. Hiker feeds, hostel hospitality, trail angels: All this trail magic has slowed down my hiking speed and my will to make miles. I'm going to blame this one on the Honeymoon Hikers and their uncanny ability to track down the luxuries of the trail.

CHAPTER 20

Magic

"Whaa—"

I'm settled in my tent for the evening when suddenly I'm spooked by the sight of a paw appearing under my tent fly.

Bear!

My heart drops to my stomach. I want to see a bear, but not this close. More like me on one mountain and the bear on another. I wait and listen for movement outside of my tent.

Nothing.

I reach through my tent opening and quickly snatch one of my trekking poles. I unzip my tent fly a few inches, stick my pole out, and swing it back and forth.

Nothing.

I wait and listen as I stare at the inside of my tent fly, waiting for the storm to break the calm. I wave my pole outside again and then slowly poke my head out.

I don't see anyth—OY!

A few yards directly in front of me, I see glowing eyes staring right at me.

Crap! Crap! Crap!

"Hail Mary full of grace, Halloween thy name, bless the fruit Jesus!" I'm too scared to remember the prayer I learned as a child from my catechism days, but I need something to still my nerves.

Wait, those eyes are too small to be a bear's. Can it be . . . a wild dog? I clap as hard and loud as I can, but the creature doesn't even flinch.

I should have known.

I was told that clapping loudly will scare wild dogs away. But obviously not for me: It stands there staring at me then suddenly storms off.

I hope it stays away. Wait—was that a collar I saw around its neck?

I'm alone at a campsite by a running stream about 100 yards from Harpers Creek Shelter. There's a hiker at the shelter, but from where I am lying, I can't tell who it is. Down by the stream, I'm secluded and alone but not lonely. The sound of water gently falling over boulders and running downstream relaxes me and drifts me peacefully to sleep.

Morning comes, and I reach over to unzip my tent. The zipper sound brings memories of my first mornings on the trail, when the campsites were crowded with tents, giving them the look and feel of a small village. I reflect back on the community of eager hikers and how small I felt in that unfamiliar world. Surrounded by highly experienced hikers, I felt as if I were acting in a role I hadn't prepared for, ad-libbing and hoping that somehow I would learn the lines along the way.

Now, after two months on the trail, the memory pulls at my heartstrings. This walk I do, day in and day out, has changed. There's no more Moving Village. Overdrive, Peach, and the Honeymoon Hikers are at least 10 miles ahead of me. Although I miss my tribe, this new solo hike doesn't feel wrong. I'm not the same hiker I was two months ago. Nature, in a way, makes more sense to me. My thoughts are clearer, and I cling to the notion that my spirit is richer too.

During breakfast, I see the dog again. He doesn't look as vicious as he did last night. In fact, he's a tiny thing, and yeah, that's a collar around his neck. *Could he be hungry?*

I think I have something for the little guy to eat. I don't eat meat, but a few weeks back I bought a packet of Spam for a hiker friend, and it's still somewhere at the bottom of my food bag. I dig it out, open it, and lay the Spam on the ground. He comes over and sniffs the meatlike product before eating it.

"Such a cute boy," I say as I reach down to pet him.

I don't know much about dogs, but this dwarfed black and brown German shepherd-looking dog with fox-like ears and a stubby tail seems fairly young.

He wolfs down the whole thing and then dashes off.

"Yeah, eat and run! I don't feel used at all," I yell after him.

I pack my gear, and before I head out, I sign the register at the shelter. The most recent entry mentions a dog with no owner hanging around last night. He was fed, and someone attempted to put a leash on him, but he didn't take to it. I hope someone is helping the dog out of the woods and back to his owner.

My morning starts with a 3-mile hike up Three Ridges Mountain. I prefer a morning climb to one that comes at the end of the day, when I'm worn down from a long haul of hiking. For me, it's easier to get the climbs out of the way when I have the energy.

An hour into my hike, as I begin a mountain descent a couple of miles from the next shelter, I see the lost dog following a hiker.

Oh, good. Looks like the pup is being helped.

As I walk several yards behind them, the dog stops, looks back as if he recognizes me, but then decides he doesn't and keeps following his new friend.

Guess he had more than Spam to offer you, huh, boy?

When I reach Maupin Field Shelter for a quick break, I see the dog's hiker pal lying on the floor of the shelter. Sitting close by and eating a snack is a female section hiker named Skillz.

"Hey, where's the dog?" I ask, as I take my pack off and sit on the shelter floor.

Then, as if beckoned, the pup rushes over to me and makes himself comfortable under my legs.

"Hey boy," I say, scratching behind his ear. "Are you taking him to his owner?" I ask the hiker, who is resting in the shelter with one arm covering his face.

He doesn't answer, so I assume he's asleep until he curtly and without looking over at me, says, "No, he just started following me."

He doesn't seem concerned for the dog's well-being—or should I attribute his dismissive demeanor to being tired? Either way, he seems to want to be left alone, and that's fine by me.

"Hey, there's a number on his collar," I say.

"What is it? I'll call it when I get a signal," says Skillz.

Great, someone actually cares. She takes the number, and I go over the register before heading back on the trail. Minutes later, the pup is behind me.

"What? You're not feelin' grumpy pants either? Fair warning, I like to talk. Just saying."

Dog continues to follow me for a few hours, and he even chills with me when I have lunch on a mountain overhang with an amazing view. He sits contentedly by my feet, unaware that he's lost.

Such innocence.

He senses that I'm staring at him and looks up at me, and at that moment I decide.

"OK. I'll get you home somehow, boy," I assure my new four-legged hiking partner.

For the rest of the day, he stays close to my side, unless he hears a sound beyond the nearby trees that I don't hear. When that happens, his ears perk up and his body straightens out, like some kind of pointer breed. He races after the unseen movement in the woods. He's quick and leaps over branches and other obstacles like a miniature deer.

I should call his owner soon; he or she must be worried.

But I wait—for what, I'm not sure.

Derick, call the dog's owner soon. He can't stay on the trail with you. Reality check: You barely planned a solo thru-hike. There's zero way you can add a dog to your mix—fool!

There's that pesky voice again. I know, I know. Still, I can't stop imagining the rest of my hike with a canine companion.

"Shoot, I don't have extra food to give you, boy. I'm running low even for myself. I only have a packet of ramen noodles and a couple spoonfuls of peanut butter. OK, let's hope for some trail magic."

At 4 o'clock, I finally call the pup's owner, but there's no answer. I leave a message, partially relieved no one picked up.

Dog and I continue our hike. He stays close behind me, when he's not running off after forest critters I don't see. We continue, but after a few minutes without seeing him, I stop. I turn around, whistle, and call for him to show himself. "Hey, boy! Come on, boy! Don't be lost out here! Come on, pup!"

Nothing.

I wait, scanning the dense trees.

Where did you go, boy?

Suddenly I hear something approach from behind. I jump with a scream, "Bear!"

"Damn it, boy. You scared me. I almost sharted."

I lean over and pet the stealthy dog, glad he's safe and also that he's not a bear.

For the rest of the hike, he stays in front of me. The trail bends ahead, and I lose sight of him, but when I make the turn, he's waiting until he sees me and then continues. I check my cell phone and notice I missed a call. I listen to the voicemail. "I hear you got my dog. Call me back." The voice is stern, and I'm taken aback. I guess I expected a gentler voice, or perhaps the voice of someone elated that I found his missing pup. I'm not thrilled with his choice of words and his harsh tone. It sounds as if he's accusing me of kidnapping his puppy. I call back, hoping I misinterpreted his tone.

"Hello," I hear a voice say on the other line.

"Hi. I called earlier about your dog."

"Yeah, where are you?" he asks abruptly.

"Well, I found your dog at Harpers Creek Shelter on the Appalachian Trail. I'm going north to Rockfish Gap in Waynesboro tomorrow."

"Oh, OK—um" he hesitates.

"Can you pick him up there?" I ask, a bit annoyed at his lack of concern for his dog.

Aren't you eager to reunite with this cute pup?

"Um, I don't know. I have to work," he says.

What? I found your dog! Why aren't you thrilled? What is wrong with you?

All this runs through my mind, but I keep it cooler than Steve McQueen. "OK, well, can you find someone to pick him up?"

"Um, no. My girlfriend works too," he stammers.

I pull my phone away from my ear and look at it in disbelief. I now dislike this irresponsible dog owner.

"OK," I say to give him a moment to correct himself. I'm still hoping he will recover and prove to be a worthy caretaker of this dog.

But "I'll call you back" is his response.

I want to tell him not to bother, that the dog is staying with me.

"OK, I'll be here," I say instead.

He calls back a few minutes later, agrees to meet me tomorrow at 10 A.M., and then hangs up without expressing even a hint of gratitude.

"I see why you ran away, boy," I say.

I'm filled with doubt, but I move on, my four-legged companion taking the lead. We reach a trailhead by a road where a trail angel has left a few gallons of water for thru-hikers. I begin to fill up my water bottles. Lunchtime is approaching, and I start to wonder if my companion likes peanut butter, but before I can test his taste buds, he races toward an older couple climbing into a convertible car.

"Hey, boy, come here," I call, but he charges on.

Damn it, boy, let them be.

I finish filling up my bottles, then rush after the dog. By the time I reach him, the couple has set out a makeshift bowl with water for the overly friendly dog. I apologize for the disturbance, but they show no sign of being annoyed. I explain the situation.

"He'll be safely home first thing tomorrow," I say, but my inner voice doubts my words.

Before they leave, they give me food that they didn't use for their day hike. I thank them and wave goodbye as Dog and I watch them drive off.

"Dog, I wish I was returning you to them. They were nice, weren't they?" He looks up at me in agreement.

"You know, I can't keep calling you Dog or boy. With your skill for getting trail magic from strangers, like the Honeymoon Hikers, I think I'll call you Magic. Yeah, your trail name is Magic," I say as he looks up at me with those adorable puppy eyes.

Damn you, pooch! I'm not supposed to get attached to you. You're going back to your owner.

My inner voice warned me not to get too close to this canine. *You don't need the heartache,* it said. Still, what do I go ahead and do? I give him a name.

Yeah, you're in for some hurt feelings.

We continue on, and as we hike, I share with Magic the long story of my AT journey: my inexperienced start, all the groovy hikers I've met, and what I've learned along the way.

"There was this spooky female hiker. She was pretty, but she looked possessed. I thought she was going to steal my soul or something, but she ended up being cool. Simple mistake."

When I stop talking to catch my breath, Magic looks up at me as if to say *I'm listening; continue.* I do. He's a good listener.

By late afternoon, I scan my Awol guide for a secluded camp area. Magic is overly friendly, so to avoid irritating other hikers, I think it best that we camp alone. We stop a mile away from the shelter at a decent camp spot a few yards from the trail. We eat dinner; I give Magic the trail magic tuna he'd yogi'd from the couple earlier today. As I settle in my tent for the night, Magic curls up just outside my tent fly. We're both tuckered out, and don't find it difficult to fall asleep.

In the middle of the night, I hear Magic growling at something that must have been lingering too close to us. I ease back to dreamtime, knowing I now have a watchdog to keep away the nocturnal creatures in search of my delicious body parts.

A 7 A.M. start has us moving quickly past a shelter and arriving at Rockfish Gap a half-hour ahead of schedule. I sit on a railing by the road with Magic lying under my legs. While we wait, I think about our shared hike. Like me, he's a bit inexperienced, but I can tell that, with some training, he'd be the perfect companion for a long-distance hike.

I stand up and stretch my legs. I rest my backpack on a low stone wall as I lean against it and stare out into nothing. Magic, without a word from me, obediently stays by my side. I've never owned a dog before and now I'm wondering why. Why have I deprived myself of such devotion, such pure loyalty?

Something catches my eye, and I look to my left. A short distance away, down the road and breaking through a thick fog, I see a white pickup truck approaching. It passes us then turns around back to the side of the road where we stand.

"I think . . . I think that's you, Magic," I say with a lump in my throat.

My mind is clouded; I can't think straight. Then my heart sinks to my stomach as I see what look like several small cages in the back of the pickup.

It can't be.

A lanky-looking guy with straight greasy hair steps out of the truck and walks over to us. The uneasiness I have been feeling since the moment I spoke to this guy has increased tenfold.

Returning Magic is the right thing to do.

But somehow it feels like the worst thing I could ever do to a living soul that I care about. Every fiber of my being is against handing my friend over to this stranger.

Still . . . .

"Hey," I say to the man.

He nods. I don't like him. I look down at Magic.

"Here you go, boy," I say with a heavy heart.

He stares up at me either clueless or ignoring the fact that we have to part ways now. I want to grab him and run down the street, escaping the villain in this drama we find ourselves in.

"Go, boy. Don't you recognize your owner?" I say, the words feeling dry in my mouth.

Does Magic recognize this guy? Is that why he doesn't want to move from my side?

The stranger suddenly bends over to pick up *my* dog. I instinctively start to reach for Magic, but I hold back from grabbing him and running back into the woods.

"He's a good dog. What breed is he?" I ask.

"He's a mutt with some Belgian malamute in him."

"Oh, well, how old is he?" I ask another question, but it's not the one I really want to ask.

"He's a pup, five months old," he says.

"Ah, I knew it," I say quietly, trying to hide my sadness.

As if wanting to know everything about Magic before he leaves my life forever, I open my mouth for another question, but I'm quickly stopped short.

"Well, I have to go," he says. He turns and marches toward his truck.

He opens one of the cages and shoves Magic into it.

I'm sorry, boy, I'm sorry.

I watch the white truck drive away. I have the strongest urge to run after it. *How much for the pup? That's all I had to say. Why didn't I . . . .*

Forget that I'm not prepared to hike with a dog; I could have figured something out. I should have tried. Now I'll never see Magic again.

I don't move. Moving will only make this real and end my time with Magic. I stare off in the direction of the white truck. Even after it disappears into the fog, I continue staring, waiting for something to happen that will make this all right. My face feels warm, and my eyes threaten to reveal my sorrow with tears, which I angrily fight back. After a moment of hopelessness, I take a deep breath, turn around, and walk back to my pack.

"That wasn't right. That wasn't right," I say to no one. A hiker who happens to be standing there waiting for his ride into town turns to me and watches in silence. "Not even a thank you or a ride into town," I say. "I mean,

I didn't return him for that, but still . . . ." I stop talking for fear that I may weep uncontrollably.

Magic, what did I do?

It begins to rain, but I just sit on the railing without my friend. I'm alone—and this time I'm lonely.

CHAPTER 21

Boots & Melody

FOR 101 MILES I WAS RELIEVED OF ANY CONCERNS I MAY HAVE HAD ABOUT running low on food, thanks to five rest stops, termed *waysides* along the portion of the AT that passes through Shenandoah National Park. Most waysides have a small restaurant or a lunch counter, as well as a grocery, camp supplies, restrooms, and drinking water fountains. This scenic section of the Shenandoah Valley is a favorite to hike, but some hikers rent inflatable rafts, kayaks, or canoes to *aqua-blaze* down the Shenandoah River instead of hiking the actual trail.

I choose to stay on land and I'm glad I do. It's my last day through the Shenandoah section, and it is a wondrous one. Rays of sunlight illuminate the wilderness around me. The leaves are charged, as if animated with displays of endless shades of green. Against the brilliance of the sun, the tops of tall trees dance their subtle dance. Their bark, dappled by sun and shadows, creates colors I have never seen before. I look up at the outstretched limbs of the surrounding trees, reaching toward the limbs of their neighbors, creating a roof of greenery over the trail. Where the branches do not meet and block the light, the sun's rays break through, touching my face with their warmth.

By 3 P.M., as I reach the road that leads to Front Royal, Virginia, I see a couple of hikers from Switzerland I recognize from my last days with the Moving Village. The couple is known for playing instruments and singing throughout their AT thru-hike. They're a good-looking pair. The man, in his mid-thirties, is tall, lean, and athletic in appearance, a former professional volleyball player. His companion has short black hair, wears glasses, and is considerably shorter than her partner. Both have Swiss accents, which I find charming and pleasant to hear.

"Boots and Melody, right?" I ask as I approach the two, who have just strapped on the heaviest-looking packs I have ever seen on a human being.

"In the flesh," says Boots.

They just resupplied in town and are headed to Jim and Molly Denton Shelter. There's a solar-powered shower at the shelter, which provides my motivation for the day. I'm eager to wash some sweat off my body.

I converse with the couple for a while until I notice they are bent over from bracing the weight of their resupplied backpacks. They look as if they're each carrying a cannon—aimed at me. My groin muscle is straining just watching them stand there with all that weight.

Mindful of their discomfort, I excuse myself.

"It's cool, we do this all the time," Boots says. "Instead of taking our packs off, we stand with them on and continue talking."

We promise to continue our talk when we get to the shelter.

"You go on ahead. Our resupply is slowing us down," says a smiling Boots.

"OK, see you at the shelter," I say, moving swiftly on with a backpack that suddenly feels light as a feather.

Goodness, those packs were gargantuan.

I arrive at the shelter, where a few hikers are eating dinner at a picnic table under a pavilion.

"Hi, where's the solar shower?" are the first words out of my mouth.

"That way, past the shelter," one of them says, pointing over his shoulder.

Sweet.

"The water may be cold. It's been cloudy all day," he adds.

"I'm OK with that, thanks."

I drop my pack and rush over to inspect the outdoor shower. On the way, I pass the shelter itself, which sports a large porch with an Adirondack bench.

Well, that's a first. I dig it.

I reach the entrance of the shower.

Oh . . . .

I'm not sure what I expected, but it wasn't a barrel over a privy-looking stall with no door or shower curtain.

I pull on the rope attached to the barrel, and a shower of water is released.

Good enough.

I run back to my bag, set up my tent, and head to the *privy shower.*

As I return from my cold-ass shower, Boots and Melody arrive. Melody quickly begins pitching their tent, and Boots starts unloading his pack on the picnic table.

I grab my mini stove along with my food bag and walk over to the picnic table, where Boots is in the process of making dinner for the two of them.

I set up my alcohol stove and begin heating water. I glance over at Boots and his culinary arrangement. What I see looks like something out of a busy Thanksgiving Day kitchen. Spread out on the picnic table are a large cooking pot, a frying pan, and a cooking gas tank of a size I've never seen before. I glance over at my compact stove, where water boils for my simple ramen noodle dinner, and it looks pitiful in comparison. Boots's side of the picnic table, which is most of the table, is covered by a bag of oranges, a bunch of bananas, vegetables, spices of all sorts, a large ziplock bag full of trail mix, and much more. He has enough food for a hiker feed. It's definitely not your typical thru-hiker setup.

How do they do it?

My curiosity is running wild.

"Um, is that a skillet and a spatula?"

"Yeah," he smiles. "What, you don't carry one?"

"I uh, no . . . , " I say.

Boots looks at me expectantly, as if knowing what I'm going to ask. "We decided we're not going to compromise the way we eat just to lighten our backpack weight," he explains.

"Oh, OK," I say, and then I catch a glimpse of Melody setting up what looks like the Legion of Doom's headquarters.

"Whoa, do you guys sleep on the first or the second floor of that duplex?" I ask Boots.

I'm not exaggerating when I say I could probably fit three or four of my tents into that mansion. "You guys are living like royalty."

"We need the space. We keep it busy in there," Boots says with a wink.

"I've never seen such a tent," I say. "Do you have neighbors over for tea?"

"We take in a few thru-hikers," says Boots.

"Man, who carries what, and how heavy are your packs?" I ask.

"I carry the food, and she carries the tent. We're not sure of the weight," he says. It's hard to tell who has the better end of the carrying deal.

Boots continues: "She sets up the tent, and I cook. Like when we're at home, she wears the pants, and I wear the apron in the relationship. If something is broken in the house, she fixes it, and I prepare the meals for her."

Melody, hearing our conversation, nods in agreement. I now want to be their best friend.

The next day we camp at another shelter together. They set up their fortress behind some trees, not far from my tent. In the evening, just as everyone settles into their tents, I hear a song coming from their New York City brownstone tent. I can't tell what language it's in, but it sounds beautiful.

"Goodnight, everyone," they say in unison.

"Goodnight," I say to my Honeymoon Hiker replacements.

My night is as peaceful as ever, and when I wake up, I half expect Boots and Melody to be standing by my tent singing me gently awake.

"Morning, Boots," I say, approaching him as he's making breakfast at the picnic table.

I assume Melody is breaking down their townhouse.

"That was a lovely song last night. Thank you for the serenade."

"You're welcome. It's a traditional song from the nineteenth century. We only sang the first and the last verse," he replies.

"Man, it was nice. You know, I wish I could be sung to sleep every night."

"Well, if you end up camping where we are, then you'll hear it again," he agrees.

"Done. Where are you going today? Never mind; I'm not letting you guys out of my sight," I say in jest, but a small part of me does want to follow them to the end of the trail.

A few miles into the day's hike, I return from a quick break at a shelter. As I turn back onto the AT, I see Boots and Melody taking a break at a small campsite clearing.

"Mr. Fabulous, we're living the life," exclaims a joyful Boots.

"Yeah we are," I reply as I settle next to them. "It's nothing like New York City. When I stepped onto this trail, it was like crossing into a portal to another dimension."

"Yeah, this is a big change for you," says Boots.

"You don't even know, Boots. Out here, I'm able to have long and complete thoughts. When I'm in the city, if a creative idea pops into my head, like a short story or a poem, there always seem to be interruptions. I'm often up late working on them, because one, the new ideas keep me up like a hungry newborn baby, and two, that's the time when I have the fewest distractions. But out here in the great outdoors, nothing is pressing, nothing is more important than walking on the trail. Out here all I do is hike and think, think and hike. I'm not up all night writing or reading, trying to tire myself to sleep. Man, I've actually had the best sleep of my life out here.

"To be honest," I continue, "before I began, I wasn't even sure if I liked hiking. I just knew that I wanted to get from Georgia to Maine. Once I started, I fell in love with it. Now it's something I will do for the rest of my life."

Our talk goes on for a while before I get back on the trail. I always feel rejuvenated after talking to Boots and Melody, but the hike to Blackburn Trail Center Hostel takes longer than I expect, and with no snacks left, food is all I can think of.

Now I'm here at Bears Den Hostel, and I am hoping to buy something for lunch, but the place is closed and does not reopen until 5 P.M. It's 3 P.M., my food bag is empty, and I'm running on fumes. I rest on a stone bench, staring at the lodge, which has been built to resemble a stone castle.

I dig it.

I contemplate whether to journey on another 8 miles to Blackburn Trail Center Hostel or stay here and wait for two hours until this castle lets down its drawbridge. I've only hiked 9 miles today, and I still have hopes of catching up to Big Foot at Harpers Ferry, so pushing on takes precedence. I take a deep breath as I swing my pack over my back and start to hike on. Just then, I see a father and his two sons, 7 and 9 years old, whom I talked to on the trail before arriving at this hostel.

"Look, Dad, it's Mr. Fabulous," I hear his youngest say.

"Mr. Fabulous, we meet again," their dad greets me.

"Hey, guys, long time no see," I gleefully respond.

"My boys now want to thru-hike just so they can get a cool name like Mr. Fabulous."

"Ha, that's the only reason I'm thru-hiking," I say with a wink. "Maybe you can thru-hike with them when they get older?"

"Possibly. We've been hiking this area together for a while," he says, looking down at his boys.

His sons' eyes are glued on me, so they don't notice the proud look their father is giving them.

"Do it—it will be such a bonding experience," I say, moved by the thought of their possible time together. I turn to the boys. "Hey, when you finally thru-hike, if one of you guys wants to take the trail name Mr. Fabulous, I won't mind. I may be too old to even care."

"Thanks, Mr. Fabulous," the 7-year-old says, with the type of cute high-pitched voice I find adorable in kids.

I wave goodbye, and with newfound energy, I head for Blackburn Trail Center.

Who needs energy bars?

———————

Twenty minutes later, I'm in need of an energy bar. For the gazillionth time, I check the outside pockets of my backpack for a forgotten Snickers, protein bar, or anything edible—crumbs, even—but once again I come up empty. I began the day without any snacks, which is something I never do. I'm fairly good at stretching out my food until the next resupply.

The more I think about my lack of snacks, the hungrier I get.

Oh, boy. Did I make a mistake by not waiting for Bears Den Hostel to open?

I arrive at a trailhead, where I see a crew of four repainting white blazes.

"Hi, guys, touching up the blazes? That's nice," I say in greeting.

"Yeah, we can't have you thru-hikers getting lost in the woods. We have enough wild animals in the wilderness. Where are you headed?" asks a lady holding a paintbrush and a plastic container of paint.

"Blackburn Trail Center. I'm close, right?"

"You're 7 miles away," she replies.

"Nah, are you serious? I thought it was closer for some reason. Are you sure?" I ask, depleted of strength and food.

"I should know. I run it," she says. "But you're in luck. There will be a hot meal waiting for you."

My stomach grumbles at these lovely words. I find it difficult to hide my hunger and exhaustion.

"Hey, my name is Chris," says a tall skinny guy in his mid-twenties. "I'm one of the caretakers. If you want, you can slackpack there. I'll give you this small pack I'm wearing, and we'll put yours in the truck."

My worn-out body language must have said yes because he begins to take my pack off. For a split second I give in, but then my instinct takes a strong hold of my pack.

"Um, thank you, Chris. I want to, but . . . I think I'll take it with me."

I can't believe I just said that.

I'm so tired. But I haven't been without my pack for this entire thru-hike. It would feel strange not to have it with me now.

"Are you sure?" he asks.

I go back and forth in my mind a few more times.

"No, I'm sure. Thanks," I say, forcing a defiant voice.

From the moment I hike away from them, all I can think of is the dinner awaiting me at Blackburn Trail Center. With every passing moment, my hunger increases and my pace decreases.

I should have surrendered my pack.

I reach the Virginia–West Virginia border. I ought to be thrilled, especially because it's also my 1,000-mile mark, but hunger and weariness eclipse any good feelings. I rest my forehead on the wooden marker and take in what I can. My only thought, though, is that I have *4.8 miles to go*, and that may as well be 100 more miles. I'm that dead tired.

"Whoa!" I almost fall.

Hunger has me feeling sluggish, and I'm stumbling over pebbles. Like a zombie in need of brains, I drag myself closer to food. Finally, I reach a sign that directs me to Blackburn Trail Center. I follow the endless switchbacks down. Exhaustion makes the final 0.2-mile side trail feel longer than it actually is.

Where is this hostel? Oh, I hope I'm going the right way.

Doubt turns to relief when I finally see a large house with a wraparound enclosed porch.

Walking across the driveway, I see Carol, one of the caretakers I met on the trail 7 miles back. "Hey, you made it. Go right on in," she says.

I walk up the steps, enter the porch, and see a hiker eating a large plate of spaghetti. Next to his meal, I spy a can of beer. I set my bag down and thank the hiking gods that I finally made it.

Damn, that was the longest 7 miles ever.

Chris, who I wish I had given my backpack to 7 long miles earlier, greets me.

"I'll heat up a plate of spaghetti for you," he says, his host skills sharp and ready.

"Oh, wait. I'm a vegetarian," I say nervously.

All this way, and I may not have a meal because years ago I had the genius idea to become a non-meat eater. My mother, who cooks some form of meat with every meal, couldn't or refused to understand why I would do such a thing—and now I'm pondering the decision myself.

"Not a problem; we have sauce without meat," he replies.

"I want to kiss you," I joke, but I truly feel love for this kind man.

"Would you like a beer as well?" he adds.

"Oh, yes, please, and I don't need the veggie version."

I walk over to the picnic table and settle next to a hiker I've seen along the trail. He introduces an older thru-hiker he's talking to, but hunger pangs prevent me from remembering his name. I sit quietly, listening to the two thru-hikers and stealing glances at the kitchen door. Finally, I see Chris walking over with a large plate of spaghetti. Fork ready in hand, I nearly hit the plate before it reaches the table.

Prior to the AT, I had some form of dining etiquette—napkin on lap, elbows off the table, chew food—but that's not me at this moment. I dive in, spin the spaghetti around my fork, and almost choke on the amount I try to jam down my throat. I'm trying to steady my pace when I'm interrupted by a stinkbug that lands right in the center of my meal. I stare at it for a second, flick it away with my fork, and continue eating. I realize that I should have exchanged or cleaned the fork, but at this moment I don't care. My raging hiker appetite has me doing things I would never have dreamed of in the so-called real world.

Truth be told, that bug is lucky I didn't eat it.

Just as I finish demolishing my dinner, Boots and Melody arrive from their hike. Boots gives me a gaze that says, *What the hell was that?* I can tell the trail did a number on them as well. They look as exhausted as I felt when I first arrived at the hostel. I give the war-torn couple the spaghetti meal news, and in return, Boots gives me another look, this time one of bewilderment.

"Yeah, you heard me right: food. So, take your packs off and relax at the table over there," I say.

Now that I'm fed, my thoughts are clearer, and my joy of life has returned. Boots and Melody place their bags down and head over to the picnic table. Within minutes they're served a plate of food. They waste no time eating, but they are much more civilized than I was.

That's 'cause they carry an entire produce section in their backpack and never run out of food.

While they feast, I explore the grounds. When I return, I see they're done eating, and Boots has discovered that Chris has a guitar. Soon we are sitting on the porch singing songs. Well, *they're* singing. I'm captivated by Melody's angelic voice.

This Swiss singing couple are American country music fanatics.

"Do you guys know Kenny Rogers?" I begin to sing "The Gambler," clapping along.

"No, we don't sing Kenny Rogers songs," Boots says, cutting me off. Melody, beside him, chuckles.

"What? My mom played his album all the time when I was a kid. His songs are kind of catchy, no?"

"No, we still don't sing his songs," Boots says sternly, giving me an *Are you kidding?* look.

I open my mouth to begin a "Lady" verse, but Boots takes hold of the guitar and begins to tune it, and Melody begins a song. I gladly shut up and ready myself for some real music. Sitting there listening to Melody sing and Boots strumming the guitar is an experience I had hoped I would have on the AT. I lose myself in their songs. Someone says it's 10 P.M., way past *hiker midnight*, but time has no meaning tonight. It doesn't matter to me if we hit *real* midnight. I want to soak this all in, to allow my soul to be coated with silky tenderness.

As a hiker named Trailboss pours a glass of Spanish red wine, he comments that he is part Spaniard. We speak a few words in Spanish as he shares his story. Trailboss and his wife, Sandy, in their mid-fifties, live in the main house. He's in charge of caring for the section of the trail from the southern end of "the Roller Coaster" (an up-and-down hilly hike that may have been the culprit for my fatigue, along with a lack of snacks) to this hostel. He's also responsible for Blackburn Trail Center and the hiker hostel a few yards behind it. Caretakers like Chris and his girlfriend, Carol, help care for the hostel and hiker needs.

Although the night grows older, the singing continues. Boots and I refuse to accept that our melodious evening is coming to a close. After each song follows a playful insistence from me. "OK, one more song," he says.

This harmonic night has me thinking like a romantic. Eventually the performance does finally wrap up. The last song is sung, and we prepare for a well-deserved sleep.

"Let's cowboy camp tonight, Mr. Fabulous," Boots declares.

"Can I sleep in between the two of you?" I kid.

"Of course, that was the implication. We like to cuddle."

For some time now, I've been wanting to sleep out in the open with nothing but a sleeping bag. That's my intention tonight, except the mosquitoes discourage me from doing so. The same mosquitoes do nothing to deter Boots and Melody; they are revved up about the opportunity to finally cowboy camp.

I lie on a bench inside the screened porch. As soon as I close my eyes, I'm out for the count. I wake up in the morning with thoughts of singing birds and flying hikers—or is it flying birds and singing hikers?

Where's my coffee?

CHAPTER 22

Do You Get a Prize for Doing It?

HARPERS FERRY, WEST VIRGINIA, IS KNOWN AS THE PSYCHOLOGICAL halfway point of the AT, and although this quaint, historical town is about 100 miles south of the actual halfway point, it's a milestone for thru-hikers because it's home to the Appalachian Trail Conservancy's headquarters.

When I first arrived a few days ago, I headed straight for the ATC office and visitor center. Freshly shaved, I was prepared for the traditional photo that is taken and added to a large binder. Poptart, a representative at the center, greeted me with the friendliest smile. He took my photo and was the perfect first person to meet in a small town I have never been to before. He made my visit to the center a pleasure. With tons of info about Harpers Ferry, Poptart left me eager to walk the small streets of this town.

Harpers Ferry is the region's epicenter for outdoor activity and sightseeing—the ideal place for me to rest, recharge, and ready myself for the second half of my thru-hike. With that in mind, yesterday I stayed for a zero, admiring the town's historical monuments and charming shops, and meeting some of the pleasant locals. The day of rest also gave me time to prepare for my next AT feat.

The quad-state challenge consists of hiking through four states—Virginia, West Virginia, Maryland, and across the Mason–Dixon Line to Pennsylvania—a total of 43.4 miles in less than 24 hours. I'm a sucker for trying my hand at difficult tasks, and this is one I can't resist. To begin, I need to hike back southbound almost 2 miles to the Virginia–West Virginia border, which I crossed two days ago.

It's 4:30 P.M. when I arrive at the border. My plan is to sleep until 11 P.M. and then start hiking by midnight. But my plan is a wash. My mind is racing, and sleep eludes me. A text from Big Foot informs me that there is a storm forecast for tonight. I'm not discouraged, though. *Perhaps now it will be a true challenge*, I tell myself.

Rain comes, but by midnight it slows to a drizzle. I pack my belongings, walk to the border sign, give it a pat, and start my night hike. It doesn't take long to realize I did not plan correctly for this challenge.

At Harpers Ferry, I picked up five care packages that contained baked goods and snacks, goodies that I refused to leave behind. As it turns out, homemade cookies and brownies are delicious but weighty. Between them and the five books I shoved in, my pack is the heaviest it has ever been, at 45 pounds. How did it not cross my mind that a lighter pack would have been the obvious way to go when taking on a time-and-distance challenge? With a pack full of fat and sugar, the only thing I'm prepared for is a face full of acne and a diabetic coma.

I hear a sudden crash in the darkness and stand frozen with fear. Whatever just ran through these woods must have been enormous, because the smash of broken branches sounds like a giant angrily kicking trees out of the way. This is my first night hike, and I now question whether I have made a serious mistake. I somehow thought I would be doing this with other hikers, making the scare factor nonexistent. This now feels like the worst idea I have had on this AT journey. It's raining again, and the fog and darkness seem to hide potential threats behind every tree.

I flash my headlamp into the black woods on either side of the trail as I hike on. Then I see it, deep in the woods: two glowing eyes following my movements.

Eek! I swallow a scream.

Before I started this challenge, a hiker felt the need to tell me that two glowing eyes facing forward belong to predators, like wild cats or bears. Most plant-eating animals have eyes on the sides of their heads.

Damn, how I wish I was ignorant to that fact.

The eyes I see are definitely facing forward. They're watching my every move.

"Keep your distance, OK?" I say politely to the glowing eyes that follow my movement along the hard-to-see trail.

I try to distract myself with thoughts of my hike through the 500 miles of Virginia. Some say you get the Virginia blues, which they attribute to the length of time spent in that state. No blues here. I enjoyed every moment of it. I made a serious effort to find what makes the state special, and without fail, I kept all forms of melancholy away.

Out of the woods, literally, I walk through the streets of Harpers Ferry, over a bridge, and across the West Virginia–Maryland border. The rain has stopped and the fog has lifted, but the pitch-black trail is illuminated only by my headlamp, which I turn off out of sheer curiosity. I wave my hand in front of my face, and blackness is all I see. I quickly turn my lamp back on; darkness is frightening for this urbanite, who thrives in the bright lights of the city.

The trail takes me under a highway bridge.

"Mr. Fabulous!" I hear someone call.

"Huh, yeah?" I call back.

Who the . . . .

I continue to move slowly forward, and as I get closer, I see something—someone—sitting under the bridge. It's Impulse, a hiker full of over-the-top stories of his thru-hike, which always seems to be going awry. His hilarious stories leave the rest of us thru-hikers laughing and also scratching our heads in disbelief.

"Dude, I'm so glad it's you. I didn't know what was coming my way," he says, then continues in his wired way of telling a story, "and I was like, I'm not prepared for this! I don't have a headlamp, so I had to crawl in the dark. It started to rain, so I stopped under the bridge and fell asleep."

None of this makes any sense, but I laugh at the way he tells his story. As usual, he races through his words as if frightened that a slower pace may cause them to get lost in his brain forever.

"Ha, it's crazy how the dark can play tricks on your imagination," I say. "I heard something ahead of me, and if you didn't call out my name, I'm pretty sure I would have wet my pants."

The plan was for Impulse to meet me back at the Virginia–West Virginia border, but when he didn't show up, I assumed he had changed his mind.

"Dude, what happened? I was waiting for you at the border," I say.

"I didn't know where to meet you. I got a ride into Harpers Ferry, so I didn't know which way was north or south. I made it to this bridge around 10 P.M. and I knew you were starting at midnight, so I chanced that you would come along sooner or later," he says breathlessly.

Impulse is known for yellow blazing—when hikers "cheat" by obtaining rides farther up or down the trail—and for getting into some strange situations. I have an inkling that his company is going to make this challenge an unorthodox endeavor for both of us.

Exhibit A: Impulse doesn't have a headlamp, so he's forced to hike close behind me. How has this guy thru-hiked this far? He's such an amusing mess.

The trail begins to get rocky, and I can't tell if my light is helping Impulse along. I warn him of big roots and tricky spots that may trip him up. The process slows me down a bit, but I mentally stay positive by thinking of how funny it was finding him under that bridge. The humor begins to fade, though, an hour into our hike when I discover he's out of water.

What! Did any thought at all go into doing this challenge, Impulse? It takes all the power I have not to voice my frustration.

The little water I provide will not be enough for him to continue much farther. We have to stop at the next shelter, which is something I was hoping to avoid. Time is ticking on this challenge, and a stop could crush my goal.

My ever-so-fabulous tolerance is further tried when I find out that the water source at the next shelter is a half a mile down a steep trail. Down and up again, that's a mile off course. I'm the only one with a headlamp, so of course I have to go down with him. I start racing to the water source, but large rocks and roots make me regulate my descent to a much slower pace. Exhausted, we rest at the bottom. While mosquitoes feast on us, we fill our containers. I'm starting to feel grumpy and a bit annoyed by the fact that if I'd hiked alone, I would have been much farther along the trail. Still, the night is young. This hoopla will not affect my time. We hike back up the AT, and for the next few hours, I try to make up some time.

By 10 A.M., Impulse's new boots begin hurting his feet.

New boots!

Even I know that racing along a rocky trail is not the way to break in new boots. This guy makes me feel better about the choices I made for this challenge. Now, of course busted-feet Impulse needs a break, so we stop at Rocky Run Shelter. There, Impulse makes what is probably the best decision he has made on this trail: He decides to end his challenge attempt. With a quick adieu, I hurriedly strap on my pack and head for the trail before he changes his mind. Ready to make up lost time, I press on, the 24 hours of no sleep doing little to diminish my energy.

———

Hours later, as I'm pumping water at a stream, a dad with two young sons approaches me. "Hey, are you thru-hiking?" the man asks.

"Yeah," I reply.

"Great, how's it going for you?"

"I'm having a wonderful time," I say. I tell him about my quad-state challenge. I smile, expecting some form of praise, but what I get is something else.

"Do you get a prize for doing it?" he asks earnestly.

"Uh . . . ." The question catches me off guard.

Where's the praise?

He sees my hesitation and continues. "Do you get a trophy, money, a prize—anything to make it worth doing such a grueling hike?"

Man, way to burst my bubble.

"Well, it's more of a personal Everest for me. I just want to see if I can actually do it. Plus, I've been on the trail for three months, and I kinda wanted to mix it up a little," I say, trying to give a convincing reply, not for him but to counteract the doubts that have arisen in my mind. I'm instantly drained of energy. The lack of sleep has me delirious, and I'm slurring my words like a drunkard.

"OK," he says staring at me as if he knows my secret uncertainties. "Do you hunt your own food out here? Because *that* would be a challenge."

"Nah, I resupply in towns."

OK, you made your point.

"Oh, well, I'll leave you to it. Good luck," he says and follows his young boys down the trail.

"Thanks. Happy trails," I say, but I really want to sarcastically thank him for diminishing my will to continue. Begrudgingly, I admit he has a point.

Why am I doing this?

The answer hits me like a glove slap. For the same reason I'm hiking from Georgia to Maine: *because I can.*

With 10 miles still left to go, my hopes of arriving before dark begin to fade like the now-setting sun.

Damn, another night hike.

I'm in Maryland now, and the trail is no longer dirt but is littered with rocks, which I'm cautiously stepping on. There's not a flat surface to be found, which is definitely slowing me down. My headlamp is back on, but I still can't see the trail. I stop, search for a white blaze ahead, hike toward it, search for the next blaze, and so on. At times the trail feels less like a trail and more like a dark cavern with its darkness suffocating me.

Derick, be cool.

I cross a road and walk straight into the inky woods.

Is this the trail?

I continue pushing through large fallen branches, when suddenly I come to a nervous realization that *I'm not on the AT.*

Holy basil, I'm turned around. I'm surrounded by pitch-blackness. This dredges up a childhood memory long forgotten: a recurring dream of a mystery figure in the dark that creeps up behind me and then takes a bite out of my back. Almost every night for years I dreamed about this *thing* that left my back throbbing, causing me to wake in terror. Fear would run through me when it was bedtime. I would wrap the bedsheets tightly around my body like a mummy in a sarcophagus. I wouldn't lie on my side or on my stomach for fear of exposing my back, and I'd wake tangled in the sheets and nearly hanging off the bed.

Eventually, as I got older, my night terrors disappeared. Nevertheless, at this moment, I am taken back to that childhood distress, and although I have a pack on, my back feels exposed. I'm enveloped in darkness, and if anything were to run up on me, I wouldn't notice it until it was chomping into my back. I wonder what that frightened little boy would have thought of the grown-up version of himself out here in the real dark side of his dreams.

Monkey farts, where am I? Why am I out here? Just breathe and backtrack, I tell myself.

I walk back the way I think I came from. I have no idea which direction to go until the trail gods bless me with a sign. I follow a distant glare of a car's headlights. I'm hit hard with relief when I find myself back on the road that I had crossed earlier into the dark woods.

As I drop my pack on the side of the road, a nervous exhale escapes me. I look back at the disturbing, dark trees as I bend over to catch my breath. A salty taste of sweat reaches my lips. I wipe my face with my bandana and force myself to let go of all toxic emotions. I'm safe.

For the next few minutes, I attempt to settle myself. I then survey the surrounding area. I can't seem to find a white blaze into the woods—not that I feel a need to rush back in. I walk down the road a bit before I happen upon a white blaze and a sign pointing to a hidden trail. I shake my head in disbelief at how I could have missed it as I return for my pack and start again.

I pause before entering the darkness, which feels like it's waiting to swallow me whole. I'm back on the trail, but it's still so dark and rocky. Eventually boulders replace small rocks as I take long steps up and down the trail. Even with the light illuminating each landing of my foot, I worry that a misstep could end not just this challenge but my whole thru-hike. Then, as if I willed it, my right foot and pole slip into a gap between the rocks. I quickly catch myself before I tumble forward.

Wow, that was close.

I now care less about the challenge than about making it through this night hike unscathed.

I imagine that Maryland is a fun and beautiful hike without a 45-pound backpack on. I'm bummed by that thought and instantly promise myself to return after my thru-hike for a more enjoyable experience.

It's nearly midnight, and I don't know how close I am to the border. Frustration and confusion build. I wonder how much of it has to do with the fact that I've been hiking for 40 miles straight and have not slept for more than 36 hours. Thinking of it in those terms makes it all feel so absurd. In fact, this whole four-state challenge goes against my reason for hiking the AT. When I decided to thru-hike, I left behind the need to race against time.

On the whole, my hike has been one good experience after another. Then I tackle this challenge, and it all goes awry. Unsure where I am, I begin to run when the trail turns flat again. As I cross over train tracks, an AT sign leads me into more dark woods. I take a deep breath, let out a long exhale, and steadily continue on. I try to rest my eyes, a sleepwalking hike, but I trip as soon as I close them. My legs are wobbly, and I drift to the left, then to the right. My mind is muddled. I'm in a drunken state. My only clear thought is that this situation sucks peanuts. Feeling hopeless, I move on simply for the sake of moving.

I see another sign. I stare at what I hope is not a mirage, then tear off my pack, drop it on the ground, and embrace the Mason–Dixon Line sign with tears of joy, relief, and frustration. It has been more than 24 hours of strenuous hiking. I fall to my knees with my head slumped down, nearly touching my lap.

"I . . . didn't . . . make it," I painfully whisper to myself, as if the words are searing my throat. "Man, I didn't . . . . What was I thinking? Why did I need to do this?"

Doubts of reaching the more important sign in Maine begin to creep into my consciousness. A tear lands on my knee. A wave of anger warms my face, only to be replaced by despair, and as quick as the two emotions come, they retreat, and a calm settles over me.

I'm such a fool. Still, it's done—and I'll never, ever have to do it ever, ever, ever again.

I force myself up and continue along the trail. I reach a stream, pitch my tent, and prepare for what I'm sure will be a comalike sleep. I try to formulate a clear thought about why I put myself through such a hardship, but nothing seems to make sense. With exhaustion taking control of my brain, the only reason I can come up with is that, after it's all said and done, I did hike more than 40 miles straight. Isn't that something?

Do I get a prize for doing such a challenge? No.

Do I care? No.

Part 4

NEW SUMMITS

CHAPTER 23

Make It a Gallon . . . Now That's a Challenge!

WITH THE HARDEST PART OF MY HIKE BEHIND ME, I NOW TURN MY attention to my next destination: Pine Grove General Store. Host to the far more pleasant half-gallon ice cream challenge, the store is just past the actual halfway point of my thru-hike.

After completing the quad-state challenge, I assume I'll spend the day lying in my tent recuperating. But at noon, I step out of my tent feeling surprisingly rejuvenated and raring to distance myself from yesterday's debacle.

By 2 P.M. I begin a short hike to Tumbling Run Shelters. I reason that 5 miles is enough to negate any concerns I have about wasting a perfectly good hiking day. It's a quick hike, especially after yesterday's near double marathon. I approach two large shelters, one with a sign reading "Snoring" and the other "Nonsnoring."

How considerate.

A picnic table separates the two shelters. Behind each shelter are clotheslines perfect for hanging pungent, drenched hiker clothes. Behind the shelters, on higher ground, is another picnic table under a large pavilion.

I place my bag on a picnic table and rest a while before I set up my tent. I study the grounds in front of the shelters, observing campsites surrounded by tall trees as far as the eye can see. There's a sense of serenity that generates tranquility within me. The 43.4-mile ordeal has left my mind in a weary, dreamlike state. I surrender to this feeling of ease.

After a quiet dinner with two older hikers, I head to a nearby brook. Exposed rocks jut above the water and form a crossing over the wide stream. I crouch on a large rock in the middle and begin to clean my bowl

What the—?

Magic, my canine hiking companion, has found me! The small dog takes a few steps past me. My heart sinks when I realize it's not my dog but a fawn. It looks up at me and stands there, as if waiting for a photo op. I reach for my camera but remember I left it in my tent.

Damn.

Strangely, it doesn't take much notice of my presence. I begin to wonder if it's blind, but then it makes its way downstream, gracefully jumping over big exposed rocks. I scan the woods, expecting to see mother doe watching its carefree fawn, but I don't see a thing. Magic's lookalike disappears from sight.

A baby deer practically landed on my lap. Well, I'm glad I didn't end up hiking with it. We know how attached I get to strays.

Back at my tent, sleep comes quickly, and once again I am left wonder-struck by my days out here on the Appalachian Trail.

———————

I know it's her as soon as I set eyes on her. She has a palpably mild manner, as if nothing is more important than sitting on a log and eating an energy bar, while chatting with passing hikers. She embodies the power of now.

"Are you Shanti?" I ask.

Weeks ago, I noticed that a hiker named Shanti, like me, uses the peace sign in shelter registers. I thought, "Hey, that's my thing!" until someone pointed out: Isn't the spread of peace the reason I use it?

Oh yeah, that's right.

Throughout this hike, I've read Shanti's entries. She comes across as earthy and is one of those hikers who leaves an impression with her words and actions. This is who I see before me.

"Yes, how did you know?" she asks. "Did you see me in the news talking about my Hike for Peace?"

"Nah, I left my TV at home, so I missed it," I say, smiling. "I just had a feeling it was you. I've been following your register entries for a while. I noticed your peace signs, and I'm all about that. See?" I show her the silver peace sign charm hanging from my necklace.

She nonchalantly nods and says, "Oh, OK."

She's what I expected, with a cool, chill persona. I'm surprised when she announces that she started the AT on her 50th birthday.

"Say what? You look more like 30," I say.

"Oh, thank you," she says, batting her eyes.

"Well, how old are you?" she asks.

"Now, see, you need to mind your own business!" I say, giving her my best annoyed expression.

She laughs as I keep a semi-straight face. It's something I love to do to get others going.

I move on, and as I arrive at the Birch Run Shelter, my home for the night, I get a text from Overdrive saying he's at Quarry Gap Shelters with Soho. That sets my mind at ease.

While pitching my tent, Shanti arrives. "Hey, Shanti, are you staying here tonight?"

"I think so, yeah," she says.

There's a fiery spirit about this youthful 50-year-old that ignites good energy.

"Is Shanti your real name?" I ask her. "'Cause I know one other person named Shanti. It's an uncommon name."

"Nah, it's my trail name. It's the Sanskrit word for *peace.*"

"Oh, makes sense with the whole Hike for Peace thing," I say.

She pitches her tent on the other side of the campsite. While I finish getting myself settled, a teenager, a bit overzealous with a great big smile, cheerfully introduces himself as Anthony.

"Mr. Fabulous, that's great!" he says enthusiastically when I introduce myself.

His hiking buddy, Aaron, joins him. Aaron's demeanor is a bit more reserved. He has cool, slick, combed hair and an outfit unlike any I've seen on a hiker. In fact, nothing he has on is hiker material. He's wearing a thick button-down shirt with black jeans and suspenders. He may be wearing hiker boots, but the rest of his appearance cries out *hipster.* The kid has style, but he won't survive a thru-hike wearing what he has on.

They are doing a *flip-flop hike,* a thru-hike that varies the order of the usual south-to-north route. They started at Harpers Ferry and will hike to Mt. Katahdin in Maine, then ride back to Harpers Ferry for a southbound hike to Springer Mountain, Georgia. For another variation, some thru-hikers hike from Springer Mountain to Harpers Ferry or a designated area, then jump to Maine and hike south to where they left off.

"They're trying to give me the trail name Babyface," says Anthony.

"Oh, like the singer?" I ask.

"There's a singer named Babyface?" he says, surprised.

"Yikes, how old are you?" I ask.

"Seventeen, why?"

"Yeah, you're a bit too young. Why Babyface as a trail name?"

"Because I'm a man with a baby face," he says.

I want to differ about a 17-year-old kid being a man. But I know better than to argue that fact with a teenager. He's tall with a man's body but a grade-school face that has begun seeing signs of facial hair.

"Oh, OK. Just *Baby* wouldn't work, right?"

"Nah, but I can go with *Babe*."

"That could work," I say.

I bathe in a nearby stream and retire to my tent after eating a ramen noodle dinner. The soft tunes from singing hikers at the nearby shelter still ring in my mind, along with visions of ice cream.

Half-gallon, here I come. I hope I'm not too anxious and can actually fall asleep is my last thought before I doze off into hiker dreamland.

———————

When morning arrives, I find myself hiking with the newly named Babe. He's a fast-hiking, talkative kid, which is what I want today. We get to Pine Grove General Store in no time. Shanti, who must have woken up before the break of dawn to start her hike today, is waiting on the store's front porch.

I'm thrilled that this day has come. The half-gallon challenge is a thru-hiker's ritual to celebrate making it halfway to Maine. The challenge is to eat a half-gallon of ice cream within an hour. When you're finished, you get a wooden ice cream paddle with the words *MEMBER OF THE HALF GAL. CLUB* printed on it in red lettering. It's nothing fancy, and some of the letters are cut off, but shoot, it's more than what I got for the quad-state challenge.

I finish my black cherry ice cream in 20 minutes. It's not a record, but I did it with ease. A true test would have been a whole gallon, or better yet, make it two.

I head over to the register to share how simple the so-called challenge was when I hear a familiar Herman Munster laugh. I turn quickly at the sound.

"BIGGIE!"

It's a Big Foot sighting. My giant friend lurches toward me and hugs me off the ground like a child.

"Mr. Fabulous."

"I thought you were way ahead of me," I say.

"I'm at Boiling Springs. I came back to do the half-gallon challenge and to see you."

"Man, it's so good to see you," I say, elated.

"I'm here with my friend Mike, the one I texted you about. He's been hiking with me for a few days, and he brought baked goods with him."

I shake Mike's hand, but the brownies and cookies have my full attention. Eating a half-gallon of ice cream did nothing to lessen my appetite. I swallow a few brownies as Big Foot and I catch up. I tell him that Overdrive is a day behind.

"He's hiking with Peach now," I say.

"Good. He needed someone to slow him down."

"Ha, perhaps. Hey, you know, I just missed you at Harpers Ferry. You left a few hours before I arrived. It's crazy how you've been moving, doing 20 miles every day," I say. "You weren't doing that with the Moving Village."

"We're doing a zero today then headed to Darlington Shelter tomorrow. Where are you?" he asks.

"I'm doing 3 more miles today. Tomorrow, with the trail being so flat, I can do a 26-mile day and join you for dinner at Darlington Shelter."

"Do it. Catch up already."

"I will," I say, determined.

"All right, eat some more cookies," he says. "I'm going to get a half-gallon of ice cream and see what I can do with it."

With my ice cream challenge met and done, I move on to James Fry Shelter. Knowing that I'll see Big Foot tomorrow, there's no sad goodbyes. Along the way, a snake stops me short with a half-swallowed squirrel hanging out of its mouth. In the middle of its dinner, it slithers right past me. A snake with a mouthful of squirrel offers no threat, so with little fear, I spend the next few minutes trying to get a good picture of the snake and the prey in its grasp. The snake turns its head to me and stares me down, and although there's little chance of it spitting out its meal and chasing after me, I decide to let it be.

Minutes later I reach the blue-blazed trail that leads to the shelter. I stop, but instead of turning right to the shelter, I go a few yards farther ahead on the AT, toward a stream. I make a right at a footbridge and follow a trail along the stream, which leads me to an unexpected, large campsite. It's a bit hidden, right near the peaceful sounds of the flowing stream. I'll be alone tonight if I stay here, which gives me a break from a crowded camp area. Not that I mind others around me, but alone time is good too. I set up my tent and then jump in the water. I sit on a large rock, letting the current run over my legs.

A perfect way to end a perfect day.

A day of challenges? More like a day of blessings.

CHAPTER 24

Can You Drown in Rocks?

HOPING TO FINALLY CATCH UP TO MY HIKING PAL BIG FOOT, I OPT for an ambitious 26-mile hike to Darlington Shelter. I'm on the Pennsylvania section of the Appalachian Trail, and although it's infamous for being a rough and rocky state, locals tell me that for the next few days, I can look forward to flat terrain. This will give me the opportunity to make up some miles.

Today's hike takes me through a green meadow and then through farmland with young, short stalks of corn that turns into endless fields of golden wheat. Larger areas of green surround the soft, grassy trail I follow. When the trail opens like this—whether into farmland, a meadow, a pasture with grazing cows, or a bald mountaintop—it evokes a childlike joy in me. It could be because I'm from the city, where space is limited and my daily views are of buildings, but my head seems to erupt in revelry whenever I step out from the dense woods into the openness of the world. I'm tempted to drop my pack and run out into the field swinging my arms, happy to be alive.

By 2 P.M., the trail leads me through a small town called Boiling Springs, where a beautiful lake is fed by 30 natural springs. It's a sunny day, perfect weather for hiking, but today I decide to ditch my ambition and lie on a grassy area by the lake. Thoughts of reaching my destination are forgotten. What I intend as a short break turns into 45 minutes—and promises to be much longer when an insulated tote full of ice-cold beer arrives in the parking lot.

"OK, if I leave now, I'll make it to the shelter by dark," I proclaim as I ready my backpack for another 14 miles of hiking.

But then I happen to turn my sights to the nearby trailhead and see Shanti. *Dang, she must have done 20 miles up to this point.*

It's 4 P.M., and my desire to move on has dwindled significantly. This is a well-documented side effect of beer trail magic.

Ah, Big Foot, I was so close.

I take my pack off and grab another beer.

Guess I'm hanging a little bit longer.

Shanti joins the trail magic, and I hand her a beer.

"Have you seen the Traveling Musical Flip-Floppers?" she asks, referring to the singing-hiking trio of Babe, Sam, and Aaron.

"Yeah, they hiked by a few hours ago. They're headed to Darlington Shelter," I say, still partly yearning to reach my old friend.

The gathered hikers discuss whether to get pizza and share a hotel room. I could try to resist the allure of a hot, cheesy, delicious pizza, a shower, and a soft bed, but why? One of the great things about the trail is that you can go with the flow and change up plans as you please.

The next day, after a restful night at Boiling Springs, I finally hike the 14 miles to Darlington Shelter. This section of the trail, with its wooden stiles, takes me over fences and leads into green meadows that slow my pace to a near crawl. The grassland has a hypnotizing control over me, like the poppy field in *The Wizard of Oz*, and I'm slow to leave its trance.

It's nearly dark when I finally do make it to the shelter and see Shanti.

"Have you met Catnap?" she asks, pointing at a hiker with curly black hair and a rounded brown beard.

He resembles a character out of a biblical story, with a knowing look and a calm demeanor.

"Who, you mean James, brother of John, over there?" I ask.

"What? Oh—yeah," Shanti says, either ignoring or not getting my reference. "He just got back on the trail after having Lyme disease."

I'm impressed that he returned to finish his thru-hike. Contrary to the misconception that bears, snakes, and other humans are the biggest dangers out here in the wilderness, I've come to realize that this disease is the real threat. Too many hikers have fallen ill due to tick bites. I want to stroll over and commend him, but it's getting dark and I'm currently nursing my own condition: laziness. I settle comfortably into my tent. I'll meet this apostle of the AT in the morning.

But when morning breaks, I'm back on the trail while Catnap is still in his tent. I'm usually the last to leave camp, unless it's a nero into town—that's when I get my ass moving faster than Overdrive ascending a mountain. It seems like every hiker in the area plans to stop by the Doyle, a cheap hiker hotel with a bar and food, so I'm sure I'll see him there.

The trail goes through Duncannon, Pennsylvania, and when I get there, I pass the Doyle and go straight to an ice cream shop I saw in the Awol guide. I walk back to the Doyle and enter with cone in hand and a big smile on my face.

"You can't come in here with that," says a mean-looking lady behind the bar, pointing at my delicious treat.

Not the greeting I expected.

"Oh, OK. I'll finish it outside," I say.

I do an about-face, exit the bar, and place myself on a curb. Sitting like this reminds me of a childhood moment in the streets of Brooklyn, waiting for my turn at our neighborhood kickball game. Without a care in the world, I finish my ice cream cone and then reenter the Doyle. The tough barkeep eyes me up and down. I stop at the threshold, raise my arms, and show both sides of my hands, as if performing a magic trick and revealing that there's nothing up my sleeves.

"See, I ate it all," I say. I open my mouth to emphasize the fact.

She gives no indication that she cares or is amused.

I see that I'm going to have to work for this one's affection.

The Traveling Musical Flip-Floppers are here with Shanti and a few other thru-hikers. It looks like a private club for smelly hikers. I greet everyone as I sit at the bar, ready for a drink, a meal, and a chance to make Stone-Face behind the bar smile.

Though I do hope she notices me soon before my hunger and thirst get the best of me.

My stomach grumbles, and I feel like a man stranded in the middle of a desert. Whether it's meat or not, I want to devour whatever is emitting that delicious smell from the kitchen.

After what feels like an hour but is probably more like five minutes, the barkeep glances at me over her glasses. She looks like a tough gym teacher with a baseball cap worn backward and a T-shirt a few sizes too big.

"Hi," I hear myself say in a wee voice.

I give her my biggest smile, which probably comes off more like a frightened stare. She gives no indication whether she likes or doesn't give two poop stains about me, but she takes my order. After checking my ID, she finally serves me a cold beer.

I order a veggie burger and when it arrives, I forgo chewing and nearly swallow it whole.

After I inhale my meal, I head over to a table by the front door with my fellow thru-hikers.

"Catnap is staying here. He said he knows you," says Shanti.

"Catnap? Hmmm. I think I would remem—"

Just then, I hear the bar door open and in he comes, looking like a disciple of Jesus.

He looks familiar, but . . . .

"What the—Mike!"

I stand and embrace the hiker I shared my first evening with on the trail.

Of course, he's Catnap.

I remember his cool, mellow demeanor and how he took a nap as soon as we got to Springer Mountain.

Damn, it's good to see him again.

"So *you're* Catnap," I exclaim.

"And you're Mr. Fabulous. You have to explain that one to me," he says with a smirk.

It feels as if I'm reunited with a long-lost brother.

"We have half a journey to catch up on," I say.

We sit at the bar and talk about our thru-hikes thus far.

"Yeah, after the bear stole our food, Josh, Swiss, and I just drifted apart."

"Hey, Mr. Fabulous," says Sam, overhearing our conversation. "Swiss was at James Fry Shelter. He said that you named him."

"Yeah, I guess I did," I say.

I didn't think that *Swiss* would stick as a trail name, but I'm glad it did. Because I still don't remember his real name.

A couple of hours later, I'm ready to part for a nearby campsite, but before I go, the stern bartender gives me the smile I worked for. She may be strong-willed and have a gruff demeanor, but it actually wasn't hard to break through her icy exterior and expose her soft side.

It's early morning, and I'm at 501 Shelter, famously known for its pizza deliveries. I walk into the cabin-like shelter to sign the register. Babe is still asleep, but Sam is up and packing his gear. Aaron unexpectedly ditched his hiking partners and hitched a ride off the trail, taking with him some of the useful items they were sharing.

"Hey, Mr. Fabulous," Sam says.

"Good morning, Voice of Reason," I respond.

Sam looks up at me with a blank expression. Last night Shanti and I talked about how Sam tempers Babe's childlike, crazy notions with more sensible plans. He's a *voice of reason.*

"That should be his trail name," proclaimed Shanti.

So, this morning, I decide to try out the trail name on him. It feels like a good fit for him.

"You know, that has a nice ring to it," Sam says.

Several minutes pass while he turns the trail name over in his mind. I can almost see the gears in his head revolving.

"Well, introduce yourself with it today, and see how it feels," I say. "But, let me say, One: It suits you; and B: It's an awesome name."

He smiles. "Yeah, it is."

With that, another trail name is bestowed. I finish my register entry and head out with Babe and the Voice of Reason.

What the frack!

The ankle-rolling rocks are bad enough, but I don't need these damned gnats flying into my ear canal, up my nose, and doing kamikaze dives into my eyeballs. I don't understand why a bug would want to fly into my eyes, where they'll just die. At this point, I can't recall when the trail was *not* rocky. I'm cautious with every step I take. My head is down, and I only look up every so often for a white blaze. Bugs stick to my face, and I want to scream to release my frustration, but before I can, I'm poked in the eye again.

Where's the relief?

I happen to check my phone and notice I have a text from Shanti: *Can you drown in rocks? Because there is an ocean of them before me!*

I look up. My line of sight reaches nearly 100 yards, and all I see is a trail covered with large, scattered rocks. There isn't a safe flat surface to step on.

It does look like an ocean of rocks.

I sigh. I could easily feel myself suffocating in these waves of dangerous ankle breakers. But I manage to keep my thoughts positive.

"Fuuuuuu-dge!" I nearly sprain my ankle. "Pennsylvania, why do you fight me so?"

I've read register entries maligning this state. Nicknamed Rocksylvania, there's little love for this part of the Appalachian Trail. I understand the frustration, hurt, weariness, and whatever else these rocks evoke, but as long as I'm on the AT, I refuse to think such negative thoughts. I may *fall* down, but I will not *feel* down. I'm not hiking through this state feeling miserable.

Still, my toes are getting numb from all the rock banging.

With the trail so rough, I'll do anything to keep myself positive, and the two teens I find myself hiking with today seem to have the same idea. Their singing is a good distraction, one that immensely entertains me, especially when Babe and Voice of Reason sing popular commercial jingles. I sing along with them the best I can before we're interrupted by the rocks on the trail.

Half-exposed rocks of various sizes cover the trail, as if they are growing up from the ground like plants. The flat surfaces on some rocks face at an angle, which makes them unsafe to walk on. Stepping over a rock with slanted sides may create a risk of landing on a sharp-edged one just ahead of it, thus turning your footing in an unintended direction.

I think back on my first day of hiking in this rocky state, when I asked Pennsylvania to be kind to me. I have lived here, so we have a history together. But no matter what I say, she continues to act like a disgruntled ex-girlfriend. I'm not sure what I did to offend this lover, but I refuse to let it sully my feelings about the beloved Appalachian Trail.

"Ouch! Son of a Brooklyn Bridge." I bang my toe hard.

Pure thoughts . . . pure thoughts.

CHAPTER 25

An Un-bear-able Hike

I SLIDE ON MY *CHANCLETAS* AND STEP OUT OF MY TENT, INTO A COOL morning breeze. A light drizzle greets me as I turn my head up and welcome the rain's gentle touch on my face.

"Good morning," I greet the rain.

I step on the trail just before 6 A.M. It's an extremely early start for me, but I'm still a half-hour behind Shanti. But soon I'm confronted with a wooden ladder against a rock wall. The rain has picked up, and I'm wearing boots that have lost their traction and are falling apart with every step I take.

What can go wrong?

I carefully climb up the ladder, studying every step and grip before I put solid weight on it. I make it to the top after only one off-balance move. Hoping I left the worst behind me, I continue. I soon learn, however, that rock ridges don't give two farts whether I make it across upright or on my back. They are not only slippery but are also steep, with nothing to grab on to for support. After slowly walking down a few wet ridges, another wet ridge diminishes my hope for a flat trail. The rain comes down harder with every step I take. I'm at least grateful for my early start as I continue with cautious steps.

OK, all good.

I slip and land on my backpack.

OK, not good.

I stay seated on the wet rock and examine my body for injuries.

Nothing broken or dislocated. I'm fine—I think.

I carefully lift myself up, walk safely to the end of the rock ridge . . . and then my legs slide out from under me. I land hard on my keister.

Sonofa—ouch!

I typically enjoy these large-rock-ridge hikes, even the steep ones, but with the rain making my footing so slippery, it's hard to find anything enjoyable about them today. I climb up another ridgetop and look down at one more slick, 30-foot descent. I grab a nearby branch for support, but it breaks in my hand. I grab another one, and it too begins to snap. If I let go of this branch, I'm going to fly right off this ridge and end up in another state. I stand there, surveying the area for a safe way down this slippery waterslide, but I see no way out of this fix. I have no choice but to let go of the branch and take a step forward. *BAM!* I instantly drop to the stone ground.

Soaked, sore, and filled with disbelief, I slide on my butt down the end of the long slope. There I get to my feet, only to slip again. If this weren't happening to me, I would think it was *haha-larious*, but right now my throbbing ass doesn't find humor in any of this.

Damn boots!

After two long hours, the rain finally stops, the sun comes out, and the trail begins to dry out. I walk across a flat rock surface without taking a spill and descend into a dense area of greenery, where a fallen tree blocks my way. I look around for a white blaze but see none.

What did I just do?

I must have made a wrong turn somewhere. I backtrack up the ridge when, out of nowhere, about 20 feet away, I see it before it sees me. A bear sitting with its eyes closed, lazily chewing on some grub.

Oh, no.

My previous bear encounter flashes through my mind: An eating bear with its back to me is startled by my presence. I run, he runs, and since we both run in opposite directions, I live. That evening I ran into camp thinking we were all done for, and even after several hours had passed, I imagined the beast pacing around our campsite, waiting to eat the first hiker to fall asleep.

The lessons from that encounter now race through my brain:

- Don't sneak up on a bear while it's eating.
- Make your appearance larger than the bear's.
- Make loud noises to scare it off.
- Don't run.
- And lastly, just avoid them.

This bear is my closest encounter thus far. If I run now, I'm surely not going to escape its grasp. With its eyes closed and its full attention on chewing, it has not yet noticed my presence. I back away slowly, down the ridge and out of its sight. I then begin banging my hiking poles together. *This will scare it away.* Satisfied that I've made my presence known, I climb back up. When I reach the top, I see that not only did the bear not run away, it has in fact moved closer to me.

Man, more lousy advice.

Making noise may work for others, but not for Mr. Fabulous, the bear toy.

OK, make myself seem bigger.

I raise both of my poles to give myself a larger appearance. The bear stares at me and then takes another step forward. I clap my poles together and stomp my foot forward in an attempt to scare it away.

Where am I getting all this false information? Did this creature just grin at my foolish antics?

I begin to take off my backpack so I can defend myself, or more likely to run like hell, but I decide against it.

I can't leave my backpack. I just resupplied.

I continue backing up until I hit the large fallen tree that prompted me to question my whereabouts moments earlier.

Why is this here?

I need to climb over the tree, try to get it between the bear and myself. I look back at the slowly approaching bear. It doesn't seem to be in a hurry to kill me, which is good. I scramble over the tree like a toddler crawling up a step. I look back again and see the bear tilt its head, as if bewildered. I must look like a buffoon. I want to cry.

Keep your cool, Mr. Fabulous. Remember: Don't run.

I flip myself over the tree, stand up, stumble, and if not for large, fallen branches on the ground, I would run. I move farther into the woods, bearing right and around the ridge, hoping to find a way out of the unmarked woods. I step into a small clearing and scan the tree— *yes,* a white blaze. All I need to do now is follow it north, and I'm safe. Well, I would be, if I had any sense at all. I turn and quickly follow the trail south, so I can hike the part of the trail I just missed. I go up a small incline where the trail follows the ridge to the spot where I made the wrong turn. As I correct my course, I see the bear back at the spot where I first saw it—and now it is a quick bear-jump closer to my jugular.

I thought I had lost the beast, but it must have been following my movements from the top of the rock ridge. This time, I whimper a little inside as I briskly walk down the trail, while the bear gazes curiously down at me. I grab my camera and suppress the turmoil I feel inside as I snap shots of the bear watching me.

The stories of bears scurrying away from humans are a joke to me. "Oh, they're like overgrown, scared dogs," is a senseless remark that I will rebut for the rest of my life. I crave the company of other hikers, and after several miles, I do see one and stick to her like glue. But sticking to Shanti is not as easy as I expect. The day's mischief is not finished with me.

A blinding headache pounds my skull, as if my brain is trying to break it open and escape. I can barely see the trail through my half-closed eyes. Sweat the size of dimes falls down my face, further distorting my vision. I can't finish a short climb without stopping to catch my breath every three steps.

What is happening to me?

My legs feel rubbery, and my mind is cloudy.

No, no, no. I can't have heat exhaustion.

I thought I was drinking enough water in this sweltering July heat, but I'm definitely dehydrated. I drink all the water I have, but it may be too late. I have to sit. I can't see or breathe steadily, and it's too hot to continue.

Where's Shanti?

I'm not getting a signal on my cell.

Damn.

I have one short climb and a descent to reach the next trailhead to meet Shanti. It should only take me 15 minutes, but it has taken me that long just to start the climb. Or so I'm guessing—I've lost all sense of time. Before I start the ascent, I rush behind some trees to release the contents of my bowels. I get to the false summit, but then I have to rush once more behind a tree to empty what is left in my system. When I finally make it to the top, trees spin around me, and I fall over. I lie on the ground for an undetermined time, hoping someone will come by and see me sprawled on the trail, but no one does. I remove my pack and attempt to stand. Hunching over as if punched in the stomach, I puke all the water I attempted to hydrate myself with.

Yup, it's too late. My body is rejecting water.

I lie back down on the trail, face up. Vomiting was probably the best thing that could have happened. The throbbing headache has subsided, and the trees stop spinning. I look straight up, and through my sweat and tears I see a blue sky. Memories of a younger me run through my mind.

"What color would you like your room painted, Derick?" Mom asks.

"Sky blue," I respond.

I'm not sure why as a 5-year-old I chose that color. I liked the sound of it, but perhaps even in my child's mind I also sensed that being in a blue room would plant the seed of a limitless sky. That image would transform into the mantra for my adult self.

"The sky's the limit," I whisper to myself.

I slowly sit up and grab my cell phone from my bag. It has a few bars.

"Shanti . . . ."

"Fab, what's going on? I've been trying to call you. I was getting worried. Are you OK?"

"Not really, but I'm feeling better. I'm headed down now," I say, trying not to sound as bad as I feel.

Earlier during the day, Shanti and I found a note on a tree offering unbelievable trail magic—a hearty meal, laundry, and a bed—at the next trailhead.

"Well, I'm here with John, our trail angel," she says.

"Apologize for me. I didn't mean to make him wait."

"No need, he understands. Just be careful coming down."

"OK. See ya in a bit," I say.

All right, Derick, up you go.

I slowly stand up, check my health status, take a deep breath, exhale, and then strap my backpack back on. As I descend to the trailhead, thoughts of my first week on the trail, when I would carry 4 liters of water in my Platypus and two Powerade bottles, brings a smile to my face.

I was so green.

But look at me now, dehydrated and in danger of getting heatstroke.

Have I learned nothing?

When I finally make it to the trailhead, Shanti and John are sitting on the tailgate of his SUV.

"Sorry, guys, but I almost died," I say, forcing a weak smile.

John grabs my backpack and places it in his truck. I hop into the back seat without another word—and drift off to sleep.

"Knock, knock. Fab, are you up?" I hear Shanti ask.

I'm lying on a sofa bed in our host's office. He'd offered us a meal, but I couldn't even keep down the salad. I sat staring at it for a while, unable to believe my luck, before I excused myself.

"Yeah," I respond.

"Feeling better?" she asks, handing me a Powerade.

"A little. The Powerades are helping."

"Well, Susan is a veterinarian. She says rest and lots of electrolytes are what you need right now."

"But I'm missing out on a full-course meal. A thru-hiker refusing food, that's a new one," I say, a bit peeved at myself.

"It isn't you. It's your body rejecting solids. John and Susan said if you get hungry during the night, help yourself to the leftovers in the fridge."

"That's nice of them."

"Don't worry, Fab. They understand. There's lots of ice cream. Can you try that?" Shanti asks.

I sit up and give her a hopeful look. "I guess that's the least I can try to do for our host," I say with a weak smirk.

Shanti returns with a bowl of strawberry vanilla ice cream.

Damn, I hope I can keep this down.

After my second bowl of ice cream, Shanti returns with a third.

"Well, I'm going to head downstairs and eat some more," she says, turning to leave.

"Hey, Shanti," I say, catching her halfway through the door.

"Yeah?" She turns back around to face me.

"I think today may have been the worst day of my AT life. The slippery rock ridges, another bear encounter, and the heat sickness. I can't believe all that happened today; it feels like many days packed into one."

The day's events play in my head. I could have done without all of it, but a part of me feels stronger for having gone through it. Today was the adventure I knew this hike would be. It was a challenging day, but it was an

AT experience I can share. I can do, however, do without another bear following me through the woods.

"Fab, I think the bear is your spirit animal. They act uncharacteristically around you."

"Could be. Still, I wish my spirit animal was a harmless chipmunk. Scratch that—they have annoying singing voices."

"Well, I'm glad you got that whole chasing-after-the-wildlife thing out of your system," Shanti says as she exits.

"Yeah, but there's still a moose waiting for me farther north," I proclaim.

"Don't start, Fab."

CHAPTER 26

Back in a New York Groove

OUR TRAIN IS NEARLY AT NEW YORK'S PENN STATION. FOUR MONTHS have passed since I caught a southbound train to Georgia, but the many steps taken from Amicalola Falls to New York have mentally altered those months into years. What have I missed while I was gone? Was I missed? Did New York City notice that one of its lifetime inhabitants has roamed far from home? I'm a tad overwrought by my arrival; my expectations have my mind racing. I literally walked away from that way of living when I left the streets of New York, but here I am, tempting the net I escaped from.

This city has me wrapped around its finger. No matter how far away I go, I always seem to return. But spending so much time on the Appalachian Trail has changed my ideals, and I'm unsure how I'll acclimate when I set foot on the familiar streets. The inner peace I've found on the trail, and the affection I feel for it, differs from what I feel about New York. I miss my city friends, but I'm not so sure about the city itself. Will I quickly revert to the hectic pace of the Big Apple, or will I retain some of the serenity I found on the trail?

When I first planned my thru-hike, I was going to avoid stopping in NYC, worried that the desire to stay home instead of returning to the trail might be too great. I realize now that was a thought developed with little knowledge of how the AT would affect me. The Appalachian Trail gives me all the feels, so the possibility of not returning is far from my mind.

We reach Penn Station, and when the train doors open, the current of people pulls me along. We move like a herd of cattle in a hurried, tight formation to the nearest escalator. I'm not surprised, and it only takes a split second for a switch inside me to turn on before I'm moving with determination, darting through the crowd. It's hot, and all the bodies around me make it a few degrees warmer. The stench in the air makes a familiar impression on me. I'm back in the grit of this loony megalopolis. I get ahead of the pack, moving toward the subway. Then it hits me.

Oh snap, Shanti!

I look over my shoulder and see my hiking, now city, companion not far behind me. I was so caught up in being back in a fast-paced New York groove that I forgot I wasn't traveling alone.

I wait for Shanti to catch up.

"Hey, uh, the crowd carried me away," I say. I shrug my shoulders and make a face as if saying it wasn't my fault.

She shakes her head and moves her lips into what may pass for a smile, except I get a sense that she's not down with the drastic change in me or the environment. We move on, and this time I walk at Shanti's pace.

I wake to a honking horn outside.

Huh?

My pre–Appalachian Trail morning greeting returns. Instead of singing birds and the stirrings of camp, I'm awakened by a car alarm and the sound of a crying baby. The trash truck I hear outside is a rude reminder that I'm no longer on the AT.

By late afternoon, Overdrive, Peach, Babe, and Voice arrive in the city and join us for a hiker bash at a tiki bar in Midtown Manhattan. Not long after we arrive, Big Foot and his hiking partner Big Naranja show up. The hiking group of Gribley, Pants on Fire, Daystar, and Tatertot stroll in minutes later. By the time Catnap and his girlfriend join the party, the bar is packed, and everyone is having a good time. Throughout the night, several of my New York friends arrive to join in the festivities.

"Mr. Fabulous, huh?" Nina says with a smirk.

I know that look of hers, which mingles trickery, mockery and—oh, snobbery. I knew that she'd pick up on my trail handle. Hard to avoid when the hiker group I'm with keeps using it to address me.

"Yeah, it is sooo me, right? I'm thinking of keeping it when I get off the trail."

"I'm not going to call you that," Nina proclaims.

"Aw, come on." I whine for effect.

"Nope."

"What about shortening it to Fab, like Shanti does?" I suggest.

"Don't hold your breath."

Oh, well. I tried.

"How's the whole bathing in rainwater coming along?" she asks with her wisecracking smile.

"Cold, but at least I don't stink."

She sniffs around me like a hound. "You sure about that?"

"Maybe it's the aftershave you put on your upper lip," I retaliate.

"Or more likely it's the birdbath you gave yourself in a puddle. Didn't you say you were going to bathe in whatever water you found?"

"No, yes, but—you suck," I surrender.

She laughs a laugh that I have come to find snide but have also missed.

"Why don't you come up to Bear Mountain and hike with me for a few days?" I ask.

"I got a better idea. You go on ahead and hike your pretty head off. I'll so look forward to your next blog entry of all the wonderful outdoorsy stuff you are doing," she says, feigning enthusiasm.

I give her the evil eye. "OK, well what about for a day?"

"Not gonna happen."

"First you won't call me by my trail name, and now you won't hike with me. Way to be a part of my journey," I jest, feigning disappointment.

"What? Did you dislocate your brain or something? Who housed you while you planned for the trail? And who sent you nice care packages, oh and who—?"

Damn, she has a point.

"Hey, your hair looks stunning," I say. "Did you get some Japanese straightening done again?"

She swings her hair over her right shoulder and strokes it smooth.

"Well, actually I did get a little somethin' done," she says in a posh but drunk British accent.

Distraction never fails, like a dog with a stick. It's too easy.

Gene joins us. "Hey, D," Gene says as he puts his arm over my shoulder. "Did you hear that they're going to name a cocktail here the Mr. Fabulous?"

"Really?" I say excitedly.

"No, not really."

Some things never change, and I'm glad of it. Although my New York friends tease me about my trail name, they have followed my adventure and learned something about life on the Appalachian Trail. In a way, my hike has become their hike—kind of.

Tonight, I have my New York friends and my Appalachian Trail friends together in one place—my two worlds joined in celebration of this marvelous life of ours. If only this time together could last longer than a few hours. In a few days, though, I will pack my gear and head back into the wilderness.

New York City will always be waiting for me, but for now I belong to the Appalachian Trail.

CHAPTER 27

Strange Things on the Trail

AFTER A WET AND CHILLY HIKE, I MEET UP WITH SHANTI AT MOM'S CAFÉ in a nearby town in Massachusetts. A server just finishing her shift gives us an 8-mile ride to Eastern Mountain Retreat Center in a hamlet called Great Barrington. We're dropped off at a dirt road a half-mile from the retreat. A sign says no cars allowed, so we're forced to walk the long driveway. The large property is in a secluded area just outside of town. Dense woods surround us, changing the light to a gloomy grayness. I look up in search of the missing sun, but it refuses to shine. I get an uneasy feeling as we trudge closer to what we're hoping is our sanctuary.

We continue for what seems like a long time. I begin to wonder if we're going the right way when I hear a bark and then see a lady in her late 60s approach us. She introduces herself as Reverend L. Rose, the owner of the retreat, and leads us to our refuge.

We turn onto a dirt lane that leads to where our *oasis* is hidden. It's surrounded by trees and a field that could use a gardener. Weeds and dead plants decorate the landscape. The neat and organized Virgo in me wants to run a mower across the overgrown lawn.

This is a retreat?

We're taken past a log guesthouse. She suggests that we keep it quiet, so as not to disturb the visitors staying there. Fine by me. I just want to get out of these wet clothes and take a nice hot shower.

She walks us around to the back of her home, where our kind belong— hiker trash, that is. There's actually a sign directing hikers to the back of the house.

Wait, wasn't there a civil rights movement against stuff like this? I want to joke, but I hold my tongue.

Still, in all seriousness, something feels off. I just can't place what it is. When we walk into the hikers lounge, she introduces us to an older hiking duo called Manfred and Comanche. The reverend begins giving Shanti and me a tour when Comanche asks if she has a vacuum.

"Yes, but I am not going to bring it down now," she says firmly.

"Well, there are mouse droppings around this table," he says, pointing at a small table that has a kitchen towel used as a tablecloth and an electric hot plate placed on top.

"Just pick up the cloth and shake it off," she says, with a tone that implies she's stating the obvious.

"It's not sanitary in a cooking area," he explains.

"Haven't you been sleeping in shelters out on the trail?" she asks, as if to say, *Why so picky?*

"Well, I'm not on the trail at this moment," he shoots back. His anger is gradually growing.

"I'm not happy right now, and I think you should go back to the trail," she replies. "I'll give you your money back."

"We have a binding contract, and if you try to force me to leave, I will call the police," he says.

Reverend Rose is disquieted and offers to shake the cloth, but Comanche says he'll do it. This encounter is way too heated for me, and I back my ass up toward the bathroom. With the door open, I lean on the sink, observing my reflection as if I've never seen the thru-hiker version of myself. I'm at hearing distance but pretending that nothing is happening. Shanti walks in, and through the mirror, we exchange a wide-eyed look.

I'm actually a bit surprised at our host's reaction; she's not acting very reverend-like.

At that moment, Comanche's companion asks the reverend, "Do you have a *zzzzzzz?*" motioning back and forth with his hand as if using a vacuum cleaner.

Uh oh.

Because Manfred is German, he's unaware that the argument started over a request for the cleaning machine he just tried to mimic. I'm grateful for his faux pas because it's so amusing that it lightens the heavy air—at least for me. I laugh inside and decide that I like Manfred. He's funny without knowing it, like a German Dick Van Dyke.

I want to explain the situation to Manfred, but Reverend Rose's seething expression warns me back. I can't read her mind, but her expression suggests that if I did jump in, she'd bite my head off.

Comanche, realizing the situation has snowballed, tamps down his anger and ends the dispute amiably. With obvious disgust, the reverend backs down and heads upstairs through a door that was a wall a moment ago until she pulled on it, revealing the opening.

"She's like a Stephen King character—she's crazy," Comanche declares when she's out of earshot.

That's it. It all makes sense now—the strange feeling I had as we came up the long dirt driveway, the neglected garden, the mysterious cabinlike home with cheap wood panel interiors that haven't been changed since the seventies.

A Stephen King character.

Picture the insane woman from the movie *Misery* as the owner of this place. Now that it has been brought to my attention, the resemblance is uncanny.

Later, I'm settled on a small rocking chair near the hidden door when I hear Kathy Bates making her way back downstairs. She's just behind the door. I rock faster, prepared to spring off the chair once she storms in with whatever sharp object she does her killing with. Instead of entering, though, she goes back up, but not before I hear her mutter to herself, "Ungrateful."

Yeah, one of us is getting murdered tonight. I'm betting on Comanche.

When she does eventually come through the hidden door, I give her my biggest smile and thank her for having us. I figure that if we're in a Stephen King novel, I'd better stay on her good side.

She walks around looking annoyed. I want to smooth her ruffled feathers with a joke, but I can't think of one that won't get me hit with a sledgehammer. So I just sit there, hoping she doesn't notice me.

Later in the evening, after the drama is forgotten, Manfred describes walking on the trail in a place where it became a deep rut with little room to place a step.

"You have to walk like model," he says with his German accent.

He reenacts model movements on a runway with his arm slightly raised up and his wrist bent. Watching this tall, old German guy making moves of a not-so-attractive drag queen has us hysterically laughing.

The next day, still alive and eager to escape, Shanti and I hitch a ride 8 miles back to the AT trailhead and then hike the easy terrain to Great Barrington, where we stay at the home of two former AT thru-hikers, Buttons and Bearwalker. We reunite with Voice, Babe, and Catnap, who are also staying there. Buttons and Bearwalker open their home to hikers each season, providing a place to sleep, shower, and prepare food in their kitchen.

I'm told that my old hiking partner Overdrive is at a nearby inn with Peach, who is sick. Shanti and I head over for a surprise visit. I knock on their room door expecting a grand welcome, but what I get is a reserved reaction from a person I don't recognize. Overdrive opens the door a crack, as if he's hiding something in the room.

"Oh, hey," he says, inching the door open and seemingly blocking my way in.

I wasn't planning on entering, but now I'm curious.

"Peach is sleeping," he says.

I heard that Peach had a fever and may have Lyme disease, so I understand his concern for her. What I don't understand is his lack of interest in seeing his thru-brotha.

"OK, well, you got a minute? Can you come out?" I ask, wondering why he didn't just step out of the room in the first place.

"Oh, yeah," he says, as if realizing that it was a good idea.

"How are you?"

"I'm good—just helping Peach through this."

"How is she?" I ask.

"I'm not sure. I think she's getting better. She's been sleeping a lot."

"Oh, OK."

There's an awkward silence.

"Did you hear about Soho getting off the trail?" I ask.

"Yeah, that's tough. But she's been sick for a while, right?"

"Yeah, she texted me saying that the doctors can't find what's wrong with her. She has some Lyme symptoms, but all of the tests they take are coming back negative. She's going to spend a few weeks with friends in Jersey, then she's headed back to Germany. Looks like it's just you, me, and Biggie left from the Moving Village."

"Yeah," he responds.

We exchange some more small talk, make tentative plans to meet again on the trail somewhere, and then say goodnight. I leave confused. I'm not sure what just transpired. What happened to my animated trail partner?

Shanti and I walk back to Buttons and Bearwalker's place.

"Fab, are you all right?"

"Huh?" I start as I come out of my daze. "Oh, yeah—just not the reaction I expected."

"Yeah, I know, that was odd. I was sure he was going to be thrilled to see you again."

"Over the top is what he's always been," I whisper to myself.

We walk in silence for a few moments before I voice a thought.

"Look, I'm aware that Peach is sick and that he's worried. So am I. That must be it, I guess. I don't know . . . ." I drift off.

Weariness overtakes me, and I just want to crawl into my sleeping bag.

"Listen, why did you guys stop hiking together?"

I look over at Shanti. She seems to sense what others don't, as if she's in tune with the Universe. Or maybe she's a witch of some sort?

"Well, we were hiking with Peach for a few days, and well, a third wheel I am not. I don't roll like that," I explain.

"That doesn't sound right. I'm sure you wouldn't have been a third wheel. What's the real reason?"

Yeah, she's a witch.

"I don't know . . . ."

"Fab?"

"Well, that's one reason. But also a small part of me, I'm ashamed to admit, felt . . . crowded."

I'm not explaining this right.

"Overdrive is like a brother to me out here," I continue, "and like any sibling relationship, at times it got . . . annoying. Day in and day out with the same person. It was still early in my thru-hike, and I wanted to do my own hike. So, when Peach came along, and I saw how close they were getting, I took it as an opportunity to move on—alone. But I still I miss hiking with him. Guess I'm being oversensitive about the whole thing."

"I don't think so, Fab."

"It doesn't matter anymore."

I retire for the night feeling sapped of energy but itching for morning to come so I can lose myself in my hiking routine.

CHAPTER 28

The Most Wondrous Trail

We reach the Massachusetts–Vermont border, where the AT follows the Long Trail for 105 miles before the AT splits off toward Maine, and the Long Trail continues toward Canada.

It's a wet and foggy day, and the rain comes and goes with no regard for us thru-hikers. Although the weather is icky, Vermont promises to be a beautiful state to hike. Well, that's what I've heard, but they sang the same song about the Smokies, which were rough and cold as a bully.

Vermont, please don't be a wicked beauty.

Catnap and I are moving quickly up Glastenbury Mountain with Shanti not far behind. We approach a piped spring just 50 yards from Goddard Shelter. Normally I filter outdoor water sources, but we are high up, nearly to the top of the mountain summit, and Catnap assures me that animals are not dropping their loads in this water source. The chances of Giardia infection are slim, but I swear, if I soil the only two pairs of underwear that I have out here . . . .

The temptation to taste a natural spring on top of a mountain is too much to resist, so for the first time on this adventure, I drink the water straight from the spring.

Oh, my.

Catnap and I give each other a knowing look. How can I describe the best water I have ever tasted? It's like biting into a moist fruit, the flavors bursting in your mouth. It tastes nothing like the tap water from New York City.

Have I not been drinking real water?

I quickly dump all inferior water from my bottles, and although there's little fear of this spring causing diarrhea, I filter what I plan to use for dinner and for my hike out of camp. I may have a carefree demeanor, but there's a limit to it, especially if it disrupts my hike every five minutes.

———————

Pine trees give Vermont a Christmas vibe, their branches hanging low on the trail. As I brush against them, the smell of Ol' Saint Nick—well, what I assume he smells like—fills the air. Fallen pine needles soften the trail. I am in a hiker's paradise.

"It's up this steep half-mile side trail," Voice informs me. I'm hiking with him and Solo, a super chill hiker in his fifties.

Damn, another climb, and a steep one at that?

The day's hike has left me exhausted and feeling out of sorts, but the scenic view from Killington, although it entails additional climbing, is the highest point on the Vermont section of the AT and is said to be spectacular.

I want to experience everything that the AT has to offer, right? I amp myself up for the steep climb.

The trail, seemingly vertical, is more like a wall of thick tree roots and rock steps. My poles would be useless here, which is why I left my pack at Cooper Lodge Shelter and brought along only my lunch. A last lunge and we're at the summit.

We are rewarded with a clear sky—our view is endless. Solo points out the Adirondack mountains to our left, the Green Mountains in front of us, and the White Mountains to our right. The peaks of New England are before us.

The view is sublime. Pine trees cover valleys, and the plumpness of mountains stretches for miles, with a carpet of dark green that is perfect in every way imaginable.

I'm so in awe of what I'm witnessing that I'm unsure whether to laugh or cry. I feel alive and supercharged. Whatever ailed me moments ago has vanished, giving way to a feeling of endless possibilities.

Now that's powerful.

———————

A nero to Hanover, New Hampshire, home of Dartmouth College, has us crossing the border to our 13th state. One more to go, with only 442.1 miles to Katahdin. I'm not sure if time is speeding up or slowing down, if this hike is less demanding or if I'm just not forcing miles. Either way, I try to keep good vibes, positivity being how I get down, yet today I struggle to hold on to that notion as the rain pours down in buckets. A trail of puddles grows into a stream that leaves nowhere dry to step. I'm forced to splash through the pools of water. The trail itself is flooded as the running water surges down, greater than some streams I've used as a water source. The rain is falling hard and loud; I can barely hear the hiker in front of me.

"Are you Mr. Fabulous?" he yells again.

"Oh, yeah! How did you know?" I yell my response through the roaring rain.

"Because you're the only black guy on the trail," he shouts back.

"Oh, OK," is my inaudible response.

Not much more to say about that, since it has become more or less common knowledge. With no other black thru-hikers on the trail, I'm guessing that makes me a celebrity of sorts. Still, right now it doesn't matter. In fact, I wish I wasn't out here in this rain. I'm moving at a snail's pace, sloshing along the trail. I turn around to see Shanti right behind me.

"All right, Fab, we're almost there," I barely hear her say.

Almost there, but I show no sign of moving faster. A wet chill sets in, and Shanti worries that we'll get hypothermia. She then says something I never thought would come out of her mouth: "We should rage."

Rage?

Shanti coined this term to describe when hikers move faster than normal, almost to the point of running. Although she often talks about other hikers doing it, I have not seen her *rage*. It seems counter to her carefree, mellow approach.

She must really want to get out of this cold, soaking wet mess we are in.

"But not downhill," she adds.

That makes me laugh. With her determination to get the heck out of this, I start the raging but almost fall over a large rock blocking our path.

"Sorry, Fab."

"No, it was my fault. I lost it when you said *rage*. But let's do it!" I shout and then start again.

I move faster than I thought possible. Shanti has given me the rush of adrenaline I needed, and she surprises me by staying close on my heels. I had no idea she could move with such speed. I'm forced to go as fast as I can to avoid being run over.

Although we make good time, we're still the last hikers to arrive at the fully occupied Hikers Welcome Hostel in New Hampshire. One look at Shanti, and I know what she's thinking before she even asks the caretaker. Twenty minutes later, he's driving us 25 miles to a busy small town called Lincoln. The drive takes almost an hour, but I don't care. I'm tired and I plan to sleep in late, followed by a zero day.

"On a dry day it's dangerous, but on a rainy day you can die," says the caretaker as he drives us into town.

What are you saying?

He points at the beautiful mountain, then continues to say that many have gotten hurt or died hiking down Mount Moosilauke. He advises that we slackpack it going south. I've been going northbound with my life in my pack for so long that doing it any other way is not an option for me. His warning comes across as a hustle for a few extra dollars when he mentions that he can assist us in slackpacking the treacherous mountain. But that may just be a fragment of my New York suspicious mind making an appearance.

When we do hike Mount Moosilauke, Shanti and I move with caution. This is the first time that the fear of slipping off the trail, toppling over a mountain, and breaking my neck has entered my mind.

The Grim Reaper will have a fight on his hands if he thinks I'm toppling over.

As I think that, Shanti wobbles, as if trying to stay upright on a sheet of ice. She steadies herself, but I decide to hike in front of her. I'd like to think that I would catch her if she fell, but something tells me she would most likely just land on me. Either way works, as long as there's a safe outcome.

CHAPTER 29

The Whites: Not Your Average Trail

AS I CONTINUE MY DAYS ON THE AT THROUGH NEW HAMPSHIRE, MY perception of this trail has changed. I've become more attuned to my surroundings. I would like to think I've gained a closeness with Mother Nature. Still, although I no longer feel out of place on the trail, faced with the sheer scale of the White Mountains, some of my early insecurities have resurfaced. Here the AT shows off how grand it is, hinting that although I'm coming to an end of this journey, I have yet to see it all.

With more than 1,800 miles of hiking under my belt, it would be fair to assume that I am accustomed to the Appalachian Trail. But my reply would be, *Shut your mouth. You don't know what you're talking about!*

The White Mountains section of the AT is not your average trail. It's not just the size of the mountains that makes them difficult but the terrain. The trail is so steep in places that if I lean too far forward while descending a mountain, gravity will pull me down to the bottom, like a mythical creature yanking me to an underground doom.

Every move needs careful study; each root you step on, each hole in a rock you grab needs to be strong and slip-free. The rocky steps are made for those with colossal stature. This vast region makes me feel miniature by comparison. I'm Jack Spriggins and I've found myself in the world of a giant.

"When we get to the giant's castle, you distract him, and I'll search for the goose that lays the golden eggs," I order Shanti.

"What about the harp that plays itself? Hold up. Why am *I* distracting the giant?"

I give her my best glare and say, "It's obvious. I'm Jack and I have to survive in this fairy tale. What do you want a harp for, anyway?"

The White Mountains pose the hardest climbing on the Appalachian Trail. We're averaging just 9 miles a day so far in the 100-plus miles of the range. The two of us are not breaking any time records climbing these mountains named after presidents, but speed is of no concern to us.

"Hey, look back, Shanti," I say, as I climb right behind her.

She turns around, and as I snap a photo, she slips and her hiking skirt lifts up a few inches.

"Whoa, you didn't take a photo of my exposed rear end, did you, Fab?"

I did not, but I don't tell her that.

"Whaa, me . . . nah . . . I would NEVER."

"Let me see the camera," she demands.

"No, come on, we have a giant to steal from," I say, backing away.

I climb back down until she stops, turns around, and continues to climb up.

When we finally do get to the top of the mountain, we don't find a giant castle, but we do see a gigantic heavenly world. This is what Earth looks like when left alone by humans. There's no deforestation, the land is thriving. I want to stay at this altitude forever, like a deity overlooking its creation and taking in the vigorousness of life.

I don't want a closer look; the view is perfect from up here.

––––––––––

Along a 50-mile stretch of the White Mountains, eight lodges, called High Huts, are strategically placed 6 to 8 miles apart. These huts, owned and maintained by the Appalachian Mountain Club, are not your average makeshift huts. They each have bunk rooms for up to 96 hikers, as well as washrooms, toilets, and large kitchens used for breakfast and summer dinners for paid guests. To keep that kind of service running, the crew members, called "croo," hike down the mountain for necessary supplies, like perishable food, and then lug the heavy packs back up the mountain to the huts.

On a daily basis, these huts also cater to a limited number of thru-hikers with something called a work-for-stay. In exchange for labor, workers get meals after paid guests have eaten and a floor to sleep on.

Shanti and I reach Mizpah Spring Hut. We've passed several huts on our hike in the Whites, but this is the first hut where we've considered doing a work-for-stay.

"What do you want to do, Fab?" asks Shanti.

Do we move on or stay? Shanti is a good sport and is willing to do either. We've only hiked 6 miles today, and she understands how I like to push for extra miles, so she has left the decision up to me.

The clouds are darkening, and rain is sure to come tonight. I'm skimming the hut's register, not altogether interested in the entries, but mulling over what to do. I have a preconceived idea that work-for-stay involves cutting lumber, heavy lifting, and subsistence farming. I'm bushed just thinking about it.

What's easier, a 4-mile hike with rigorous climbs and the threat of rain, or staying here to harvest the land?

"OK, let's stay," I finally decide.

It's early, so maybe I can get some reading done before we are given our strenuous farm duties. Cheap labor up here in this mountain hut will, no doubt, be vigorous labor.

Who will monitor our treatment? Who will demand justice if our collective bargaining agreement is violated?

"There's a library upstairs; that's where you'll stay," says a crew member. "Organize the shelves, and we'll have dinner for you after our guests have eaten."

Did I hear her correctly?

"Wait—did she mean that there's a library of hay we need to stack?"

"Books, Fab. A library of hay? What does that even mean?"

"I don't know. I thought it was another way of saying bale of hay. She threw me off."

The library room is a few feet bigger than an AT shelter. One side of the space has a low wall, giving us a view of the common room where guests are already eating. On the opposite wall are bookshelves and a few scattered books that we are to organize.

"Is this real?" I ask. "This is our work-for-stay? Yo, this is the life. I can do this six ways from Sunday. Let's do the next hut on the trail, please."

The next day, Shanti and I hike up and down Mount Washington and along mountain ridges that seem to go on for days. The weather is cool, perfect temperature for climbing, and climb we do. We make it so high above the treeline that we find ourselves among the clouds. I watch how our surroundings become coated with mist. I never imagined I would be in a place where land and sky meet. This must be how the depiction of heaven was conceived.

I'm still high off the work-for-stay Shanti and I did last night when we arrive at Madison Spring Hut, and this time I don't hesitate to ask if they have room for us. They are busy serving dinner, and it looks as if they are at capacity.

"Yes. We have a few other thru-hikers, but we can take you guys in," says a staff member.

"Great, it's on," I say gleefully.

I notice other thru-hikers at a table by a large window. We join them and together watch a colorful sunset.

A loud, overzealous band of youths and their parents shout-talk while we thru-hikers sit at our table quietly waiting. The difference between regular hikers and thru-hikers is apparent. We're exhausted from our day of hiking and are conserving our strength for more days of hiking to come. Overnighters, though, go home after their cute one or two days of hiking, so they're excited and have energy to spare.

Sometime later—perhaps an hour, I can't tell because my brain can't focus on anything but food—we are still waiting for our turn to eat. My hunger does not subside while a horde of tourists eat a full-course meal right in front of us. In fact, it's getting downright angry.

Down, boy!

Too much time passes before the common area is empty, except for myself and my fellow thru-hikers. Finally, we are taken to the kitchen, where we gather around an island work table jam-packed with food. As politely as we can, we don't waste any time. We eat as if the food will vanish at any moment and leave us with nothing. At this point, I still don't know what work we have to do. Maybe *nothing*—that would be an even better deal than last night.

I scan the mess the day's cooking has left the kitchen in—stained oven pans, dirty cooking utensils, a mountain of sauced and greasy pots in the sink. The place is a disaster, and man am I glad I'm not cleaning—oh, wait. Damn. With large rubber gloves on, I scrub at the tarry substance that is glued to the bottom of a pot.

"This one is broken. I can't clean it," I say.

"Give it here, Fab. Here, take this one," Shanti says as she grabs the pot and hands me one that looks like it will give me an equally tough fight.

"This bites. I want to be asleep."

"Are you hungry and cold?"

"No, but . . . ."

"Then zip it. We have to earn our stay."

"Hmph. You know, you're not always right."

"I am this time. You missed a spot on that pan."

"Oh." I resign to her logic and scrub away.

An hour later, we finish our indentured service. In truth, I did eat a lot, and I'll be in my sleeping bag in no time.

"Goodnight, guys," says one of the croo. "Be sure to be out before we serve breakfast."

"What time will that be?" I ask.

"Seven A.M."

Curses.

Shanti keeps falling, which slows our climb down a steep mountain. I myself am barely staying on my feet. Roots, branches, grooves on boulders, and the occasional log steps assist our descent, but that doesn't necessarily make it an easy one. Shanti grabs a thick tree branch with both hands and swings herself to the next landing. It's something she's done a dozen times, but this time she loses her grip in mid-swing and falls backward. A fall down these precipitous slopes can cause serious bodily harm, and, at first I worry Shanti is a goner.

There's no way she's going to survive this.

All I can think of for the split second of her fall is how this is going to ruin my thru-hike.

I would be expected to attend the funeral, right? Damn it, Shanti!

But she only falls 2 feet and lands safely on her backpack. She may be the luckiest creature on this mountain. I help her up and then spend the rest of our hike feeling guilty.

Glad Shanti can't read minds.

"Fab, are you OK? You seem awfully quiet and somewhat distracted. What did you do?"

Yikes—or can she?

By this point, Shanti has fallen so many times that I have my camera ready to draw from my pants pocket whenever I see her wobbling to one side. Like a gunslinger in those old spaghetti westerns, I'm ready for the shot.

Here it comes.

"Great day in the morning!" I hear Shanti yell as she falls down.

Her legs fly up in the air as she rolls headlong down a hill. She somehow slides or bounces or—I'm not sure what I just saw. She's wearing a hiker skirt, and for an instant she flashes the world around her.

I'm not close enough to her to be of any help; there are too many rocks between us for me to rush over. So, what can I do but grab my camera and start recording? Yeah, at first, a quick fright did come over me, but it passes the instant she begins to laugh. Now, I have seen some funny falls, mostly from Shanti. But this one gets the gold medal. Her slow-motion demonstration of a tuck-and-roll technique gone awry would score high in any Olympic Games.

"Shanti, what happened?" I ask as she bursts out in uncontrollable laughter.

She lies there and continues to laugh as she attempts to say something I can't make out. Her laugher is contagious, and I laugh along.

"That fall was pretty funny," I'm able to say.

"I fell perfectly," she says.

"You need help?" I ask.

She unhooks the straps of her backpack and wiggles herself free. She sits there looking hilariously disheveled.

"Looks like you had a little tumble," I say, purposefully stating the obvious.

"I don't think I have any scrapes. My pack saved me," she says as she pats her backpack.

"Can you wave to the camera, so we know that you're OK?" I ask, although it's obvious from her hysterics that this fallen thru-hiker is in great shape and spirits. Sitting on the ground with her back to me, she turns her head and greets the camera.

She begins to stand, stretches her legs. "Did you see? I was totally upside down."

"You were upside down," I say, still pointing my camera at her and recording.

"My legs were up here," she says, extending her arms in front of her at shoulder level.

She puts her left foot on a rock to examine her leg.

"Just peripheral, no blood this time," she says.

As we move on, I think of how we all fall down, one way or another. As thru-hikers, what choice do we have but to lift ourselves up, dust ourselves off, and continue along the trail, following our dream to Katahdin?

CHAPTER 30

Dear Mr. Moose

WHAT DO YOU DO WHEN YOU'RE CHASED BY A MOOSE? HIDE BEHIND A tree is the advice I've been told. Six feet tall at the shoulders and weighing half a ton, a moose is a formidable foe. But because a moose's vision is weak and its wits slow, this simple maneuver will confuse the creature long enough to end the chase. Considering my history with wild animals, though, I have every reason to believe this method will somehow prove useless.

One evening, while sitting around a campfire, a hiker told a story about someone who accidentally hit a moose with a car. The moose, unharmed but angry, used its antlers to lift the front of the vehicle off the ground and then smash it back down. With strength like that, I shudder to think what it could do to me if I did anything to piss it off. Yes, I want to see a moose, but I'm going to keep a safe distance. At least that's the plan.

On my way to Gorham, New Hampshire, I spot moose tracks on a muddy trail. I know they belong to a moose because a postcard I mailed to a friend a few days ago had a picture of a moose, and next to it was a cutout of a moose footprint.

I slow my pace, scan the woods, and wait for a moose call. I hear nothing, but I do finally spot my quarry in Gorham, when Shanti and I walk to a small grocery store and pass a life-size carved-wood moose in a grassy park.

Will this be the only moose I see on the AT?

"Shanti, take a picture of me with the moose," I say, just in case.

The next day we camp on the summit of Mount Success. It's a new experience for me, and during our approach, for the first time Shanti is determined not to stop until we reach our set destination. I'm exhausted and keep suggesting areas to stealth camp, but she won't have any of it. I hate her for the next 45 minutes. I secretly vow to seek vengeance on her, her children, and her unborn grandchildren.

We reach our campsite just before sunset, and although I feel as if I was dragged up this damn mountain like a raggedy dog toy, I have to admit it was worth it. I look up at shining stars. New York City's Times Square and its electric lights may shine bright, but it doesn't compare to what I'm seeing on this mountaintop.

Thank you, Shanti. You and your family line are safe.

"Hey Shanti, do you think—"

"No, we're not going to see a moose this high up a mountain."

"Oh, yeah. I knew that."

Morning arrives with the sun shining directly on us. We're above tree level where there's no shade, which is fine by me. The sun's radiant heat on my skin energizes my body and mind.

This beats a morning cup of coffee.

After my actual coffee, we start our day. Two milestones await us today: We'll reach Maine, our last state, and we'll hike through Mahoosuc Notch. The notch is a rock scramble that my guidebook describes as: *Most difficult or fun mile of the AT. Make way through jumbled pit of boulders.*

Two miles into our hike, we cross our last border. There are no banners to greet us, no crowds cheering us on to our last 280 miles. Only a wooden signpost that reads:

APPALACHIAN TRAIL
NEW HAMPSHIRE–MAINE
STATE LINE

← US RT. 2	16.5	
← SPRINGER MTN.	1899.8	
ME HWY. 26	14.6	→
MT. KATAHDIN	281.4	→

Shanti and I take a photo with the border sign. Our euphoria is mild compared with what Overdrive and I felt at our first border crossing. We were so elated that we spent 45 minutes taking photos with our group and eating lunch at the North Carolina–Georgia state line. That seems like fifty years ago, not five months. It's as if each step forward has added not only miles but also years—a bizarre phenomenon that I haven't been able to comprehend.

I've experienced twelve state crossings since then. Each was special in its own way, but, as they say, you never forget your first.

As I take a break in a shelter with eight other thru-hikers, we share a sense of anticipation. A mile and a half away awaits the famed Mahoosuc Notch. I imagine this section of the trail to be akin to an obstacle course at a Marine boot camp. Large boulders strewn across our path will challenge our agility, our strength, our balance, and our will.

I can't wait.

"Did you hear about the moose that fell off a cliff into the notch, breaking its leg?" begins a thru-hiker. "It was stuck between rocks. Its horrible cry went on for days before a hiker was humane enough to put it out of its misery by cutting its neck."

What kind of hiker knows how to do that? Isn't there a protective group—Fish and Game or something like that—that should have helped the moose?

That's what I want to ask, but what comes out is, "Hey, did you hear about the alien spacecraft that was found in the notch?"

I wait a beat for a response. Instead, I get curious looks.

I continue: "They say if you hike the notch at night, you may stumble upon the wreckage of a spacecraft that illuminates a marking of a dying extraterrestrial. It's a boulder with a faint luminescent print of what looks like a hand with 10-inch-long fingers. Of course, we all know that alien technology allows the battery life of the UFO to withstand time and any collision damage. This is all true, believe me."

No one believes my tale.

"OK, Fab, enough. Let's do this," says Shanti, as she swings her backpack over her shoulder.

"What's the hurry? It's only a mile long."

It's an hour into our hike, and I see no end to this notch.

The boulder- and talus-covered trail runs below cliffs that hover on either side. These cliffs are the source of the fallen boulders whose sizes vary from climbable to impossible unless we go around, under, or climb onto other smaller boulders. There's more greenery than I expected. Trees grow on every side, and their roots wrap around sloping boulders, helping us with our climbs and descents. Moss covers the tops of head-shaped boulders like toupees. In places, a stream runs in the cracks or gaps between boulders. I lower my hand close to the top of a gap and feel a cool breeze blowing up between my fingers.

"There's ice under these boulders," Shanti tells me.

"Really, even in August?"

"Yup."

What a fascinating phenomenon.

The white blazes, at some points, don't tell us where to climb, clamber, or descend.

"Is that white blaze telling us to squeeze through that?"

There's a small opening between two boulders that dips deeper into other surrounding boulders.

"Yeah, Fab, the arrow on the side of the boulder and the one over your head pointing to the opening should make that obvious. Unless you can Spider-Man your way over this wall of rock?"

I glare at her and then look up at the boulder, pondering for a second if there really is a way to climb over the smooth surface of this 20-foot obstacle.

"Fab?"

Damn, I hope I'm not claustrophobic.

"OK, here we go," I say as I remove my pack.

I turn to Shanti and add, "Maybe you should go first?"

"What, Fab? Why? You go."

"Nah, ladies first."

"Fab?"

"Look Shanti, what if there's a snake in that hole? Wouldn't it be better if you got bit? That way I could run for help."

"That makes no sense. I can run for help just the same."

"Yeah, but I'm faster, plus you had three kids. Your threshold for pain is higher."

"Move out the way. I'll go in," she says as she pushes me to the side.

"I thought you'd understand."

"No, you're ridiculous, and there's no snake in here."

I grab a nearby stick and lightly poke her leg with it.

"Huh . . . Faaaab! That's not funny," she says, laughing.

She makes it through unscathed. I then crawl in, pulling my backpack behind me. I quickly crawl out the other side, but I lose grip of my backpack and have to crawl back in to retrieve it.

"Yeah, there was no snake in there," I say, as I wipe the sweat off the tip of my nose.

We continue, and I unknowingly get ahead of Shanti.

"Fab, slow down. Stop trying to leave me behind," I hear her shout.

"It's getting shadowy out here. I'm in no mood for any alien sightings in the dark," I shout back as I sit on a boulder, waiting for her.

"Just wait there!" she retorts.

It has taken Shanti and I nearly two hours to hike through the notch—or I should say, scramble, crawl, jump, dance, joke, stop for selfies, and scan for fallen moose and spacecrafts. We are weary, measuring our steps more carefully as the dust dulls our vision. I start to feel claustrophobic in the narrow confines between massive rocks.

"Hey, guys."

I jump at the voice, which is not the one I've been hearing for the last hour and a half. I turn around and see Voice of Reason approaching behind us. It has been days since we've seen him.

"Hey, Voice. Where's Babe?" asks Shanti.

"He's not far behind."

Voice hikes the rest of the notch with Shanti and me. By now the trail is cast in shadows, the sun hidden behind cliffs. We make it into camp just as darkness surrounds us.

I have roughly 220 miles left before I complete my thru-hike, and I haven't seen a moose yet.

What am I doing wrong?

It seems that every other hiker has seen one. I have seen plenty of moose scat—way too much, in fact. When I first saw moose poo, I was psyched and even took pictures of it. When I shared my excitement with others, they shot it down because the scat was dry, proof the moose was probably long gone. I then began to see more and more poo. I inspected every one—from a distance, of course. If it looked brown and soft, I would step quietly along the trail hoping for a sighting. But if it was hard and pale, I would continue in search of a fresh specimen. After a week, the moose scat lost its allure, and my remaining days on the trail are now dwindling, along with my prospects for a moose sighting.

When I arrive at the public library in Andover, Maine, I post a blog entry with a plea to any moose that can read:

> Dear Mr. Moose, I promise not to be a nuisance if you show your-self to me. A quick picture, maybe a video. Oh, and I would like to touch your antlers. That's all. Thanks.
> Mr. Fabulous
> P.S. I'm the one with the dreadlocks.

That should set some moose events in motion.

While I hike and suck on a lollipop in the shape of a moose's head, I reflect on the fact that I have seen a moose statue and moose scat, and even heard a moose, which to my ears sounded like a combination of a mule, a bear, and a monster. I have experienced all things related to a moose, except for seeing an actual enormous deer with palmate antlers. I'm considering taking a moose tour when we reach Rangeley, Maine. Driven to a spot where moose constantly cross, the busloads of people are guaranteed to see one of the immense creatures.

Would that be cheating?

––––––––––

Our morning hike takes us to Moxie Pond. I hear that moose spend much of their time at water sources, especially in the early morning.

I hear sounds that I imagine are made by a nearby moose lingering in the trees. Shanti and I tiptoe around the pond.

"*Moose, come out to play-i-ay. Moose, come out to play-i-ay,*" I start to sing, but then realize that it doesn't sound inviting.

If I were a moose, I wouldn't want to *play-i-ay*. It didn't work in the *Warriors* movie and it's not going to work out here.

"I bet that someone's going to catch up to us and say they just saw a moose—a moose that we passed by unaware," I say.

Shanti smiles and we hike on. Fifteen minutes later, Voice shows up at the trailhead, drops his pack, and says, "Hey Mr. Fabulous, guess what I saw?"

Un-f'ing believable.

CHAPTER 31

I Don't Want to Ruin the End for You (But It's All Going to Be OK)

On Thursday, Shanti and I arrive in Millinocket, the last town on the AT for northbounders. Ole Man, the owner of the Appalachian Trail Lodge, picks us up at the Abol Bridge Campground store. The store is a few steps from the trailhead but 19 miles from town.

Ole Man gives us a tour of the lodge, which has two family suites, six private rooms, and bunks that can sleep nine on the second floor and nine more on the third. It's a big lodge, clean and well organized. The vibe from Ole Man is inviting, reassuring me that I made the right decision to rest here for the weekend prior to our final two days of hiking.

While Shanti and I settle in, we're told that Biggie will join us here after his summit tomorrow. I never caught up to Big Foot on the trail, so the idea of seeing him one last time warms my heart.

With only one thing on our mind, Shanti and I head over to the Appalachian Trail Cafe, also owned by Ole Man and his wife, NaviGator. It's a cute space, the ceiling tiles artfully tagged with the names of thru-hikers. As we eat, we look up and point at the names of folks we've met on this epic journey. We reminisce, and a sense of nostalgia envelops me. It's going to be a bittersweet weekend.

"Guess who's here?" I hear someone say.

"Biggie!" I yell down the stairs from the second floor of the lodge.

Anticipating his arrival, I hear my giant friend laughing as he steps out of the car.

"Right here, Mr. Fabulous," he says as he walks up the steps.

He's just getting back from his summit with his hiking partner, Big Naranja.

"Finally together again," I exclaim. "I told you I would catch you."

"All right, Fabulous, not quite—you haven't summited yet."

"Yeah, there's that little thing," I say in a faltering voice.

We laugh, never missing a beat whenever we reunite. Later in the evening, we have dinner with a group of fellow hikers, and for once we talk of future plans away from the AT.

"So, Mr. Fabulous, are you going to write about this adventure?" asks Big Foot.

"Nah, too boring, not enough material. Well, maybe the parts after the first month," I joke.

"Wait, but that's when you were with me and the Moving Village," Big Foot exclaims.

"Exactly," I say with a smile.

———

On Saturday, hikers gather for the annual Trails End Festival Parade, which runs through this small town. We meet at the high school, where about 50 locals and a few thru-hikers take their places. A hiker named Wiffle Chicken wears a makeshift costume. His yellow sleeping pad is wrapped around the top of his head like a top hat, and he holds a Wiffle ball and bat. He also wears a feathered boa around his neck, which makes me wonder what hiker box he got that from.

It's a quick parade through town, fifteen minutes, and it ends in front of the lodge. Throughout the day and night, we thru-hikers indulge in each other's company, walking through the little town and checking out the shops and cafés.

Sunday morning comes way too soon. After our coffee with Big Foot at the café, it's time to leave the hospitality of the town for our last two hikes of this six-month trek.

"This is it, Biggie. I have to go."

He wraps his long arms around me and gives me a giant hug. I imagine this is what it feels like to be hugged by Frankenstein.

"Good luck, Fabulous. We'll see each other again, I promise."

"Yeah, I know," I whisper.

I turn away and hop in the car with a pang in my heart.

"Mr. Fabulous," I hear Biggie call.

As we roll away, he snaps a photo with his camera. I wave goodbye and start the beginning of the end of this story.

"It's not the end but a new beginning," is what Shanti would say.

Ole Man drops us off at the Abol Bridge Campground store and wishes us luck. From here, the last shelter is a short 9.4-mile hike on flat terrain. I touch a white blaze, something I've done at the beginning of every day of hiking. It's my way of showing gratitude and respect for the markers that guide me through the unfamiliar wilderness.

The hike reminds me of the trek that the last few remaining cast members on the TV show *Survivor* are asked to do. It's a walk down memory lane, recalling the ones who didn't make it as far. I think of my first day on the trail and the three strangers who found it in their hearts to lend a hand. I'm not sure how they sensed my struggle—I didn't think I showed it—but I'm glad they did. I miss the Moving Village, my first trail family, and wish they were here to share this moment with me. I think of Magic, my trail dog for two days. The only regret I have out here is that I found his owner.

All of my milestones and challenges are still fresh in my mind. Everything I have seen and done courses through my veins like blood. I recall a quote that I read somewhere along this journey: "If you want to sound wise, go to school. If you want to be wise, go to nature."

Shanti, Babe, and I sit in the Katahdin Stream Campground ranger station. An older ranger with an air of authority sits behind a desk, and although she may have done this hundreds of times, she makes us feel as if our accomplishment is the first she's ever recorded.

"OK, I have number 437 and 438. Who gets what?" she asks with a smile.

Babe is doing a flip-flop and is halfway through his hike, so he doesn't register as a thru-hiker at this point. I turn to Shanti and give her the choice.

"Whichever you want, Shantirooni," I say.

"I like 437," she answers.

"All right. Trail name . . . Shanti, you are number 437." She jots it down on a pad and rips a copy for Shanti. "And you, Mr. Fabulous, are number 438."

Hmm—438? Can it be? I'll double-check later, but I think that's the same number I received when I registered on my first day six months ago.

The three of us settle in at The Birches Lean-tos and Campsite in Baxter State Park. Here in Maine and in other states in New England, shelters are called lean-tos. For northbound thru-hikers, this is the last shelter on the Appalachian Trail.

Babe and I set up our tents on a platform, and Shanti finds an area several yards away. We prepare our last dinner in the openness of nature. It's a tranquil evening, and I spend it reminiscing.

After dinner, I walk my food bag to the bear cables hung several yards behind the shelter. I look up and smile, remembering my struggle to make sense of the cables at Springer Mountain.

I reach over and unhook the cable from the post. How many times have I done this after that initial day? By now it has become routine. This last night mirrors my first; I want to soak it all in. I may be feeling nostalgic, yet I can't help but sense that my time on the trail has opened in me something buried under the hardness that life can create. Trust, compassion, and the love of total strangers reign supreme on the Appalachian Trail—and experiencing them has awakened this New Yorker. A Maya Angelou quote comes to mind: "When you know better, do better." I now know, and I am better for it. My time on the AT has set a course for self-improvement. It's an inspiration to experience all that life brings my way and to keep an open heart for everyone I meet.

With darkness cloaking the camp, I walk back to the shelter as John, the caretaker from Springer Mountain in Georgia that I met on my first day on the AT, approaches with a cake.

Well, I'll be.

"John?" I ask.

"New York! Surprised?" he asks with a smile.

This guy is something else—he actually remembers me. He places the cake on a picnic table, adds candles to it and asks if anyone has the book of matches from Springer Mountain that he gave to hikers on their first day.

I retrieve the matches from my pack.

"Strike the match and light the candles, Mr. Fabulous," he says.

I struggle to create a spark with the worn-down matches. But after several attempts, the match sparks a fire, and I light the candles. Pieces of cake are passed out, and we all stand around the picnic table, instead of sitting.

The night air steals my will to fight off sleep. Heavy-eyed like I was my first night on the AT, I excuse myself and settle in for my last night on the Appalachian Trail.

It's 6:45 A.M. on September 17, day 183 of my Appalachian Trail journey. Shanti and I await the Honeymoon Hikers and Voice of Reason, who stayed in town last night. Babe wanted a view of a rising sun, so he started his summit five hours earlier. I considered joining him, but the thought of my last hike being a frigid one in the dark did not appeal to me.

On the porch of the ranger's station, I read some of the final entries of thru-hikers who already made the last ascent. I'll sign it when I return with my thru-hike completed. The entries are all heartfelt. The most telling is from Catnap, who summited days ago and is probably back home in New York: *From thru-hiker to through hiker.*

"Here they come," says Shanti as three cars drive into the gravel lot.

"Hey, Fabulous, want some cake?" asks Ratman, as he exits his son's car.

Emerging out of one of the cars is the filmmaker Squatch, who is working on a documentary and will be filming our summit.

"Hey, guys, what's your total trail magic count?" I ask the Honeymoon Hikers.

"Two hundred and one," says Tumbler.

"You didn't reach three hundred? That's tough. You should consider this thru-hike a bust. Maybe next time," I say, feigning disappointment.

"Ha, maybe next time, Fabulous," says Tumbler.

"You're taking a full pack? Do you plan to pitch your tent by the Katahdin sign?" Ratman asks.

"Hun, he's a purist, remember," Tumbler says.

I can't tell if she's reminding him or being sarcastic.

"It's light," I say.

The food bag is what made my pack heavy, and now all I have are snacks for today's summit.

"Well, you definitely won't need your poles. You'll need both hands for the rock scramble," says Ratman, who's done this before.

I teeter between carrying them with me or leaving them behind. As Ratman heads to the ranger's station to sign the register, I hand my poles to him.

"OK, then would you mind placing my poles on the porch?" I ask.

"Not a problem."

When they return from the ranger's station, we all start for the finish together. It doesn't feel like a thru-hike but more like an excursion, a simple day hike with friends. We reach a waterfall 1.3 miles in, and I bite my lip with a nagging thought.

"I'm going back for my poles," I say to Shanti and Voice.

For six months, over 2,100 miles, I carried what I needed to live out here on the AT, and that included my trekking poles. It doesn't seem right to leave behind what has become a part of me, an extension of my limbs. This may be a case of the crazies, aka Mad Hiker Disease, but I want them with me on this final climb. And with that decision made, I feel better. I have been true to my style of thru-hiking, and I'm not going to change on the last day.

I hang my backpack behind the last privy on the AT and head back toward the ranger station.

I briskly hike, or more like jog, along the fairly flat terrain.

"You must have summited in the dark if you are returning already," says a day hiker whom I storm past.

"Nah, I forgot something."

I get to the parking area.

"Mr. Fabulous, the top of the mountain is the other way," says a thru-hiker sitting at a picnic table with her hiking partner.

"Ha, I forgot something."

I rush onto the porch, grab my poles, and rush back out.

It's as if I'm teasing myself. So close to my goal, I run in the opposite direction, postponing the end.

Well, I'm off again.

"Your poles? That's what you forgot? You're not going to need them, Mr. Fabulous," says the thru-hiker.

"It's a prop for my summit photo," I say with a smile.

She returns my smile, and they both express good wishes. "Congrats, Mr. Fabulous!"

"Same to you!"

With the false start behind me, I begin my summit hike—alone.

My hiking buddies are now several miles ahead of me. It wasn't my intention to experience these last few hours without them. That said, I'm now able to take in my surroundings, spend an extra moment observing the trail's bends and turns, study the distant ridge line I'll be hiking soon. I sit on a boulder, in no rush to move on. I want to milk this day, these last few hours, these final miles.

A cool pocket of air chills me like a breeze from an air conditioner. I rub the goose bumps forming on my arms. I stand and start again, and as I pass some branches, I raise my hand to the leaves, which are low enough to touch. I turn my face up and let the sun shine its warmth on my skin. A surge of strength flows through my body, forming a wave I will surf to the top of this mountain.

My pack is light, but I can tell how much easier this would have been if I didn't have it on. Nonetheless, it doesn't matter. I'm lovin' this final hike.

I picture the wooden sign ahead as I reach a false summit.

I think of all the people I met and hiked with. I wish many were here to share this day with me, but they are here in spirit.

My thoughts are interrupted by a text.

What the—I thought I turned this off. Dang, can a brotha get a serene moment?

I'm surprised that I'm even getting service. I guess I'm not as far up as I thought.

The text reads: *I told you we were going to make it! I'm several days behind you, thru-brotha!*

Overdrive. Knowing him, if he was summiting today, he would be at the famous sign by now, eagerly waiting for me. During our time together, it never crossed my mind that I would be doing this without him. That pains me a bit.

Damn.

The start of tears blurs my sight.

As I try to piece together my feelings and thoughts of my time out here in the wilderness, I've come to compare this process of thru-hiking on the AT to phases of human growth. It starts with the innocence of childhood, then moves to the awkward and stubborn teen years, then to the know-it-all twenties before reaching our later years, when we can use the wisdom of our experience to guide us. These phases, which took years to travel through in life, I passed through in my few short months of this journey. This is life in a flash.

A subtle wind blows a dreadlock across my face—no hair buff today.

I know I'm getting closer when I begin to see hikers I started with hiking back down. I greet and congratulate the Honeymoon Hikers. They're driving home and not returning to town. I missed a final summit with them, which makes our farewell that much harder. They ease my pain with a swig of their moonshine. With a hug, we say our goodbyes and go our separate ways. This feels like the last day of school; we're happy to be done but missing our friends already.

Trying to collect myself, I hike with my head down. When I look back up, I see the sign from a distance. Is it real? I have passed several false summits; this could be another.

I walk closer and stumble a bit. Physical and mental exhaustion has weakened my agility.

Yeah, it's the sign.

My chest feels like it's holding trapped wild animals that are trying to break free. The closer I get, the harder it is to contain these beasts. I refuse to look up, but of course I instantly do. I see my Lil' Fam.

I hear someone say, "There's Mr. Fabulous!"

Stay cool, stay fabulous. I chuckle at the thought.

I'm a few yards away. I stop, turn away, and cover my face, like a child making himself invisible from others.

If I can't see them, they can't see me.

In truth, I wish not to be seen. Squatch is filming his documentary, and although I don't want this captured on film, I don't have a choice. I let go—and then it doesn't matter anymore. My shoulders slump in surrender as Shanti and Voice of Reason approach me. I hug them, forgetting to fight the tears. They step back and give me my moment with the almighty wooden sign. I stop a few feet short and stare at the weathered marker.

There you are.

A warm tear rolls down my check.

I've been looking for you. I'm here. I'm finally here.

I hesitate, knowing that when I touch the sign . . . it will be done.

I walk up, lean my left forearm on the sign, followed by my head, covering my face and the tears that burst through. I forget everyone around me; there's no one but me and my unleashed emotions. Moments pass before I compose myself. I grab one of my bandanas and wipe a small area on the sign.

I then reach down and kiss the faded brown wood. I may be an emotional wreck, but I'm still fabulous, and I know that putting lips to this wood is straight up nasty.

I'm called back from my reverie when I'm told to get ready for a summit photo. I can't decide what pose is best for a postcard—yeah, that thought crosses my mind—so I let it go. It doesn't matter. Going with my emotions, I stretch my arms out in an attempt to embrace the sky.

"I did the AT," I whisper to myself as I sit on top of the world.

ACKNOWLEDGMENTS

It has been seven years since I completed my epic thru-hike of the Appalachian Trail, and now that I've finished writing my story, it feels as if it never even happened.

Did I actually hike the AT from Georgia to Maine?

Physically, I feel the same as before. Why don't I feel special? Why doesn't it feel like I did something out of the ordinary? The memories are there, yet the experience fades like a dream when you return to the "real world."

I've kept in touch with the Moving Village. I've spent time with Overdrive. In fact, I was ordained so that I could officiate his wedding to his beautiful wife, Eliza, who is a scientist at the Kennedy Space Center. To become close friends with such a genuinely good man would have been cause enough for me to thru-hike the Appalachian Trail.

That being said, friends who read *The Unlikely Thru-Hiker* before it was published wanted to know what happened to Overdrive during the end of our thru-hike. He was such a big part of my first few months of the trail, but there was little mention of him during the second half of my thru-hike.

If I could do it all over again, I would try a bit harder to find a way to hike more of the trail with him, especially the end. But it was difficult to execute. At times, Overdrive and I talk about our separate summits. Not hiking that last, momentous climb together is not a regret for me, but it's sort of an alternate ending that I think of at times. Still, we are tighter than ever. In fact, there were many late nights while writing *The Unlikely Thru-Hiker* that I would text Overdrive for specifics about our AT adventure. He has a freakishly detailed memory of the AT, recalling names of shelters, places, hikers, and various other information anyone not writing about the AT would find useless. His photographic memory was a vital reference for this book. Thank you, thru-brotha.

———————

A special thanks, as well, to the Byers family. Sam Byers, aka Voice of Reason, and his beautiful family were gracious enough to let me stay at their cabin for three months so that I could start writing *The Unlikely Thru-Hiker* with minimal distractions.

Thank you, Caroline and Robert, the owners of The Book Garden, for allowing my story to take form in your bookstore. Being surrounded by books was a perfect place for me to write.

Thank you, Laurie Potteiger and the Appalachian Trail Conservancy staff, for believing in my story and encouraging me to share it.

To all my beta readers, thank you for helping me along this part of my journey. Kristen Curry, you are amazing.

Thanks, Mark Burnett, for helping with edits.

Annie "Shanti" Wisecarver is the biggest contributor to this book. Without her, my story would never have taken off. Thank you for not making fun of my first draft.

Thank you to Jennifer Wehunt, Editorial Director at AMC for spending time with me on the phone and going over details of our partnership. Your words were comforting and your leadership made this all possible.

Thank you to Elaine Robbins, developmental editor/copyeditor. The Unlikely Thru-Hiker story flows nicely because of you.

Tim Mudie, project editor, what can I say? You and I were always on the same page. You knew exactly what my manuscript needed, even when I was still trying to figure it out. I thank you for your quick responses to my never-ending emails. Your patience and eagerness to work with me was an amazing experience. You shaped a good read into an amazing one. You are the man!

Thank you to Jon Lavalley for an epic cover. You captured the essence of Mr. Fabulous.

To everyone else at AMC Books, your belief in this book fills me with joy. Thank you for your hard work.

The biggest hug and love to Mom and Uncle Pablo. You were there when I really needed the support.

Big ups to all my fellow thru-hikers and to all the trail angels who helped me along. I may have not made it without you.

To Lindsey Elmore, I see you.

Finally, to all those patient souls who eagerly followed me through this long journey, I love you all.

————

So, who was I at the end of this journey in comparison to the person I was before my thru-hike (besides Mr. Fabulous, of course)?

Well, my belief that a determined mind can accomplish much was reinforced. Also, a compassion for the wild bloomed in me, when prior to the AT all I knew was city sidewalks. I have stories I continue to share with those who seem to never get tired of hearing them. I now have many unique friends from all over the world, not to mention my close friends from the Moving Village and Lil' Fam. Yet the biggest change is how often the word *love* comes out of my mouth. I'm able to say, "I love you," much more freely to family and friends.

Years have passed since my tears landed on that beautiful weathered sign on top of Katahdin. That was the end of a particular adventure, but the Appalachian Trail has traveled with me every day since. *The Unlikely Thru-Hiker* of the Appalachian Trail is what I was, but my dream is to turn that around. This wondrous trail is for everyone, including you.

————

Not surprisingly, upon my return, my New York friends refused to call me Mr. Fabulous, but I'm OK with it now . . . I think.

Peace, Love & All That Good Stuff!

ABOUT THE AUTHOR

DERICK LUGO had never hiked or camped a day in his life. This Brooklyn-born, New York City urbanite hopped a train to Georgia, grabbed a taxi at the station, and told the cab driver to drop him off at the beginning of the Appalachian Trail. Then he did as he has always done—put one foot in front of the other and never looked back.

After hiking for more than 2,000 miles, he now feels invincible and plans to cross the Sahara barefoot. (Not really, but when an ambitious spirit is successful, it will strive for even greater accomplishments.)

The Unlikely Thru-Hiker is his debut memoir. Find him online at: @dericklugo (Instagram), @dericklugo (Facebook), and at dericklugo.com.

BE OUTDO*RS™

Since 1876, the Appalachian Mountain Club has channeled your enthusiasm for the outdoors into everything we do and everywhere we work to protect. We're inspired by people exploring the natural world and deepening their appreciation of it.

With AMC chapters from Maine to Washington, D.C., including groups in Boston, New York City, and Philadelphia, you can enjoy activities like hiking, paddling, cycling, and skiing, and learn new outdoor skills. We offer advice, guidebooks, maps, and unique eco-lodges and huts to inspire your next outing.

Your visits, purchases, and donations also support conservation advocacy and research, youth programming, and caring for more than 1,800 miles of trails.

Join us!
outdoors.org/join

Blazing Ahead
Jeffrey H. Ryan

The Appalachian Trail is one of America's most revered resources. But few know the story behind its creation. The proposal could have died in the pages of a journal had it not been for Benton MacKaye and Myron Avery. *Blazing Ahead* tells the true but little-known story of a shared vision, the rivalry it bred, and the legacy of the men behind one of the nation's greatest treasures.

$18.95 • 978-1-62842-063-0 • ebook available

AMC's Mountain Skills Manual
Christian Bisson and Jamie Hannon

This comprehensive guide tackles the essential skills every outdoor lover should master. Beginners will learn the basics, covering gear, navigation, safety, and stewardship. More experienced readers can hone backpacking skills, including trip planning, efficient packing, and advanced wilderness ethics. All readers will set new goals, perfect their pace, and gain the tools to plan and enjoy their next outdoor adventure.

$21.95 • 978-1-62842-025-8 • ebook available

AMC's Real Trail Meals
Ethan and Sarah Hipple

Kick your backpacking menu up a notch! This compendium of trail-tested backcountry recipes gives readers a wide buffet of lightweight and nutritious meals. Adopting a practical, easy-to-follow approach, *AMC's Real Trail Meals* employs handy icons to note which recipes are vegetarian, vegan, gluten-free, kid-friendly, or require kitchen prep ahead of time. Dig into a diverse range of wholesome fare that will keep you fueled outdoors and that you can feel good about!

$18.95 • 978-1-62842-060-9 • ebook available

This Wild Land
Andrew Vietze

Almost twenty years ago, Andrew Vietze made an unexpected career change: from punk rock magazine editor to park ranger at Baxter State Park in Maine. From midnight search-and-rescue missions to trail maintenance to cleaning toilets, Baxter rangers do it all…and over the decades Vietze has seen it all. In *This Wild Land*, Vietze tells his story with humor, action, and an eye for the compelling details of life as a park ranger, making it the perfect read for outdoor and armchair adventurers alike.

$18.95 • 978-1-62842-132-3 • ebook available